Can Words Express Our Wonder?

Rosalind Brown is a residentiary canon at Durham Cathedral. Prior to this she taught on two ordination training schemes in Salisbury. She was ordained in the United States, where she lived for several years and was a member of an Episcopal Religious Community.

Rosalind is the author of several prize-winning hymns, some of which are published in *Sing! New Words for Worship* (Sarum College Press, 2004), and of *Being a Deacon Today* (Canterbury Press, 2005). She is the co-author with Christopher Cocksworth of *Being a Priest Today* (Canterbury Press, 2002 and 2006).

Can Words Express Our Wonder?

PREACHING IN THE CHURCH TODAY

Rosalind Brown

CANTERBURY PRESS

Norwich

© Rosalind Brown 2009

First published in 2009 by the Canterbury Press Norwich
Editorial office
13–17 Long Lane,
London, EC1A 9PN, UK

Canterbury Press is an imprint of Hymns Ancient and Modern Ltd
(a registered charity)
St Mary's Works, St Mary's Plain,
Norwich, NR3 3BH, UK

www.scm-canterburypress.co.uk

British Library Cataloguing in Publication data

A catalogue record for this book is available
from the British Library

978 1 85311 969 9

Typeset by Regent Typesetting, London
Printed and bound in Great Britain by
CPI William Clowes, Beccles NR34 7TL

In Memory of
Angie Simco

CONTENTS

INTRODUCTION

'The kingdom of God is at hand' is a cry that has rung down the centuries and has had world-transforming effects. God has given us good news to share. The privilege of preaching is immense. The potential impact of preaching is life-changing. The need for preaching is undiminished. And the wonder is that we are called to share in this ministry. Why, then, are so many sermons so emasculated and unmemorable? Too often they lack breadth and vision, but settle for something that is pedestrian and frankly boring.[1]

I am an enthusiast for preaching. My experience is focused on more traditional ways of preaching, and so I do not venture into print on contemporary 'fresh expressions'. But whatever the form of preaching, when we pare it down to absolute basics, it is helping people to know and love God. If we add flesh to those bones, it is about being asked to spend time reading and studying Scripture on a regular and disciplined basis, letting God transform us through the experience, and then sharing the joy of our discoveries with other people when we gather to worship. We keep one eye on Scripture and one eye on the people who will hear us, and the dialogue is, at times, fascinating. Preaching keeps our eyes open to God's wonderful ways with the world; it invites us to enter into the liturgy more deeply and be transformed in worship; and it nourishes us while we prepare to nourish others. It is an astonishing privilege.

Over the years since childhood I have heard hundreds of sermons and dozens of preachers of enormously varied quality and memorability, and during a recent sabbatical, when I sat in the pews of a different church every week, I added to that store of sermons. Many have been excellent and some have had very tangible effects on my life, but over the years I have also endured many eminently forgettable and occasionally unintelligible ones that might have been in Anthony Trollope's mind when he wrote so pithily, 'No one but a preaching clergyman has, in these realms, the power of compelling an audience to sit silent and be tormented. No one but a preaching clergyman can revel in platitudes, truisms, and untruism, and yet receive as his undisputed privilege, the same respectful demeanour as though words of impassioned eloquence or persuasive logic fell from his lips.'[2] In the last 15 years I have preached to a wide range of congregations on three continents: weekly in a parish; occasionally to students training for ordination or at student chaplaincies; on a one-off basis for congregations of all shapes, sizes and churchmanships when doing supply across a diocese, at conferences, at pastoral services; and regularly to the Cathedral congregation where I share the preaching with several other clergy. I have also tried to teach Anglican, Methodist and United Reformed Church ordinands and Reader candidates to preach. This book emerges from all this mixed experience.

It is not just a 'how to preach' book, although my role in training people to preach means I cannot ignore this, hence the final chapters discuss many practical aspects of sermon preparation and delivery for people who are beginning to preach. Sermon preparation is as much about our own preparation as it is about the process of preparing a particular sermon, so the book is about how we, people called by the Church to preach, are formed as preachers and are prepared to preach. Every preacher is first of all a baptized Christian, a member of the body of Christ, and we are formed as we live in the Church. We have a preaching heritage from the Church, so I begin with an overview of preaching through the first two millennia. When I was learning to preach I never had such a framework into which to place the insights of past and present preachers whom I read in my studies, or my own experience of listening to preaching. If we know our inheritance as preachers we can choose how to fit into it; if we don't know it we are cut loose from our bearings.

Among the many resources God gives us, the gifts of imagination and creativity are vivifying but often overlooked in preaching, indeed in our lives as a whole. We worship a creative God who used words to bring new life into being and who entrusts us with the responsibility to use words as creatively as the prophets once did. Developments in preaching in the last 50 years have arisen in part because people have used their imaginations. So I devote a chapter to creativity and imagination and also look at the liturgical context of preaching which is too often taken for granted (and therefore ignored) in the rush to find something to say about this week's Scriptures. My plea is that we take the liturgy very seriously, just as we do the Scriptures themselves – both draw us to God. The message we proclaim is that the kingdom of God is at hand, and whether we are preaching pastorally at a funeral, prophetically to the assembled great and the good, informally to a group of school children or routinely to the faithful on the nth Sunday after Trinity, our ultimate message is that God's kingdom is coming on earth as it is in heaven. God is drawing near: in Jesus Christ, Emmanuel, God is with us.

The surprise for me as I wrote this book was the way that rhetoric came more and more to the fore as an essential element in preaching. I expected it to be there in the background, but it pushed itself more and more to centre stage. As I listen to sermons, I realize that often what makes the difference between a good one and a weak one is not the underlying content but the way it is shaped into the text and preached in the pulpit. As preachers we sell ourselves short far too often, and rhetorical resources are there to help us. Barack Obama's use of rhetoric has captured the public imagination and is perhaps a contributory factor to two television series on oratory and speaking which have just started as I finish the book.[3] The Church can take note.

The preparation for preaching is a vital element of our spiritual life; it is a time of focused attention to God and to God's word on behalf of those to whom we will preach, but it is also transformative for us and a loving invitation to make time to be with God week by week. The ultimate test of who we are as preachers is how we are growing in the knowledge and love of God. I am grateful for the friendship and example of so many people who have modelled that love for God in their preaching and in their lives. This book would not have happened without the generous grant of a sabbatical from Durham Cathedral in the last three months of 2008. I am very grateful to the Bishop, the Dean and colleagues on the Chapter for this, particularly for covering my duties and for the ongoing example of their good preaching. Thanks, too, to the Cathedral community for their regular, perceptive comments about the sermons at the Cathedral, which indicate the way they take preaching seriously, and for the encouragement of their enthusiasm. Part of my thesis is that preachers must take their hearers into account, and the people of Durham make that task a delight. Colleagues have kindly given permission for me to quote from or refer to their sermons without seeing what I have written about them; all the sermons can be found on the Cathedral website (www.durhamcathedral.co.uk/schedule/sermons). Progress on the book was helped by the offer from the Revd Canon Dr Joe Cassidy of a visiting fellowship at St Chad's College at the University of Durham for the duration of my sabbatical, and by the book of *Matt* cartoons from the Revd Tony Lynn to read when writer's block set in, and to colour in if it persisted. Finally, thanks to the Very Revd Michael Sadgrove and David Gibbons, who read the draft through from their different perspectives.

I dedicate this book to the memory of Angie Simco, a close friend from undergraduate days with whom I heard many sermons and who died as this book was being finalized.

Rosalind Brown
Durham Cathedral
Easter 2009

Notes

1 It is both an encouragement and a challenge that in a recent survey of churchgoers, 72 per cent of respondents said that their favourite part of the service was the talk or sermon. See http://www.dailymail.co.uk/news/article-1177585/men-want-macho-hymns-fewer-flowers-dancing.html, accessed 6 May 2009.

2 Anthony Trollope, *Barchester Towers*, Oxford University Press World Classics, 1996, p. 52.

3 *The Speaker*, which searches for Britain's best young orator, and *Yes We Can! The Lost Art of Oratory*. Both were on BBC2 in April 2009.

I

THE WONDER OF PREACHING

When Nathan went to see King David following his hushed-up affair with Bathsheba and the resulting death of her husband in battle, which had been carefully set up to look like an accident, he had an awkward message for the king. In effect, he had to preach a sermon that involved judgement to a congregation of one. How should he do it? We know from the story in 2 Samuel 12 that he went about it in an extraordinarily effective way: he told a 'once upon a time' story about a rich man who killed a poor man's only lamb to feed a visitor (2 Samuel 12.1–4). The effect was instantaneous: David was furious and pronounced judgement on the rich man, thus enabling Nathan to turn the tables and in four words drive his message home: 'You are the man!' David immediately repented and Nathan announced God's response. In probably no more than three minutes one of the most effective sermons ever preached was delivered: it had a purpose, knew its audience, had an appropriate methodology, unambiguous content and clear delivery, it engaged its hearer, evoked response and led to godly action. What more can we ask of preaching?

* * *

What are we trying to do when we preach? Essentially we have good news of a gracious God, and gracious words are needed to bring God's love to the attention of a weary world. More expansively, we share in the nurture and formation of the people of God by opening their eyes to God's love, presence and truth. We equip them for ministry, strengthen them in difficulty, comfort them in distress, challenge them in discipleship, help them to make sense of everyday life and to notice things with the eye of faith, and we invite them to conversion of life. The cry of an unknown psalmist, 'How could we sing the LORD's song in a foreign land?' (Psalm 137.4) has echoed through the centuries from its original context of Babylonian exile and expresses the Church's request of those who preach: 'help us to sing God's song in our world today'. Future hope and present practicality meet at the heart of preaching, in dialogue with God's past ways with the world.

Preaching affects all our life, it is not just writing the text of a sermon. In the ordination service the Church of England states that priests – to whom most of the preaching responsibility falls – are 'to proclaim the word of the Lord and to watch for the signs of God's new creation. They are to be messengers, watchmen and stewards of the Lord.'[1] These biblical roles yield rich imagery for the preacher. Watchmen were charged with attentive observation on behalf of others in order to ensure their well-being. They inhabited two places – their vantage point for the behind-the-scenes work of studying, observing, interpreting what they saw; and the city itself, where they explained what they had seen so that people could respond, essentially helping them to catch the same vision. Likewise, preachers inhabit two places, our studies and the world, and have the same responsibilities. Messengers were responsible for getting the message straight and speaking it plainly,[2] but no attention was needed for crafting the presentation of the message or taking account of the needs of hearers. A more fruitful biblical image for preachers is that of a steward who is responsible to his or her master for the management of what has been entrusted by the owner. This brings a duty of personal integrity and reliability, as well as care, entrepreneurship, management and appropriate use of what is entrusted in line with the owner's purposes. The steward normally has considerable delegated power, but remains accountable to the master; similarly with preachers.

Rowan Williams describes preaching as 'the telling of good news that makes a difference' as the words of proclamation enact and enable change, witnessing to conversion in the preacher who preaches *from* conversion as well as *for* conversion.[3] Elsewhere, in a vivid phrase, he speaks of bishops in the early Church as 'carriers of dangerous opportunities',[4] an evocative image that alerts us to the transformative power of God through human ministry. In preaching we handle what James Earl Massey calls 'a mystery [that] involves us existentially, it confronts and engages and pinches us, it situates us in such a way that we know we must yield to its unmanageable strangeness'.[5] To preach is to be open to be pinched by God, open to transformation as we experience the Holy Spirit's moving upon the face of the waters in our life, hearing afresh in our situation God's proclamation, 'let there be light'. We preach what we know, what has grasped us, rather than theory. Calvin Miller describes our role vividly:

> Without passion, sermons degenerate into pointless points and commentary notes. They are mere gigabytes of information about God without a drop of red blood in them. Sermons should be dangerous, inflamed with hope and terror ... Preachers are not supposed to live safely. Put some orange construction cones and caution signs around your pulpit. Post a sign that says, 'Danger – obedience can be hazardous to your health. Listen to this sermon at your own risk.' Become what you are supposed to be – a messenger of life and death, of salvation and damnation.[6]

The one thing missing in Nathan's example as a model for our preaching is a context of worship. The Church places preaching within and integral to the worship of the gathered people of God.[7] This is what distinguishes preaching from other forms of monologue like lecturing, acting, entertaining or giving a speech. These may share some aims with preaching – imparting information, persuading, securing support, entertaining – but only in preaching is the speaker worshipping alongside those who listen and sharing their own faith in order to nurture the faith of others. It is part of a corporate and public experience in which both preacher and hearers have gathered intentionally to worship God and, in that context, one person has been given the authority to address the others present. They, in turn, are not passive but engaged with the preacher and the message. The corporate task in the sermon is to grasp the import of the Scriptures heard in the worship for life today. The Holy Spirit vivifies the words preached in the context of worship to make them efficacious – they achieve God's purposes, which may surpass anything the preacher dares to imagine. Preaching is an act of love, love for God and love for those who gather faithfully to worship; our desire is to help them to flourish as faithful Christians and we are never in control of the effect of a sermon. Research shows that both Protestants and Catholics agree that the sermon 'is the component of the church service [that] has the most important impact on your spiritual life',[8] and many people seek out churches where there is good preaching. When we preach we take on an awe-inspiring responsibility to nurture and care for others, to bring new life to those who hear and to encourage and equip them for the work of the ministry (Ephesians 4.12).

Preaching falls within the responsibilities of the wider ordained or licensed ministry. It thus shapes and is shaped by ongoing relationships with the congregation who, through pastoral ministry, may entrust the preacher with their deepest hopes and fears. Some are in great need, feeling powerless to cope with life, and yet by their act of coming to worship they are expressing their trust that God can help them and they long for words of hope and encouragement. Others bring huge life experience and perhaps impressive secular qualifications to bear on their faith, and preaching can help them to be as competent in their faith as in their secular work. Our responsibility is to help all these people in their relationship with God by putting the word of God into effective dialogue with their world at this time. Remember that Karl Barth told young theologians to read both the Bible and the newspaper, but to interpret newspapers from the Bible.[9]

Our aims in preaching will vary with the occasion and may include proclamation of good news, persuading, teaching, challenging, comforting, stirring to action, eliciting commitment, informing or convicting the hearers. At heart the preacher's main task is, as Timothy Radcliffe puts it, 'to help us discover every text as a cause of joy. Augustine says of preaching, "The thread of our speech comes alive through the very joy we take in what we are speaking about."'[10] One brisk definition of good preaching is that it is to the point, addresses issues of critical importance to the lives of the hearers, suggests a mission or plan of action, features a disciplined and reasonable use of time, and ends when it is finished.[11] It is not just an academic explanation of the Scriptures but is an act of proclamation designed to plant and cultivate God's word in those who hear, thus it should be *effective* dialogue that bears fruit. That fruit may be growth in the Christian life, in the fruit and gifts of the Holy Spirit, in the impact of the gospel on society, or in any other manifestation of the kingdom of God coming on earth as it is in heaven. Preaching is not merely a focus on the Bible, although there can be no Christian sermon without Scripture; neither is it merely a focus on the needs of the congregation, although these will influence the sermon. It is not oratory for its own sake and, in contrast to a lecture, where people come to hear a speaker on a pre-announced topic, in preaching, both preacher and people have their gaze focused elsewhere, on God. In essence, when preaching we are daring to put God's word into our own words – Gail Ramshaw says that 'God is speakable in the vernacular.'[12] Another way of putting it is that the homily or sermon 'is the act that, beyond all odds, allows an ancient text from a foreign culture to be received as God's Word today, relevant and powerful. Homiletic preaching transcends mere repetition of sacred formulas to become the means for God to act today', and our responsibility is to help people to make sense of the world in light of a ritual text and to make sense of a ritual text in the light of the world.[13] This can only happen if we are totally immersed in God's words and adept with our own words, having the wisdom and skill to interpret the former in the language of the latter. Preachers stand at the interface of our heritage of the biblical tradition and a world yearning to know God's unchanging power to transform and bring life. We may preach only to those who gather in church, but they will take the gospel into the rest of the world.

Preaching is never an isolated event: it occurs in the context of the ordered reading and hearing of Scripture in worship, within the daily or weekly continuum of worship. This immersion in the Church's ongoing worship means each sermon is both a one-off event and an element of a bigger whole which transcends time and space. The Holy Spirit is ever-present, breathing life, enticing and disturbing both preacher and people into more godly living. The seventeenth-century French preacher Bishop Bousset said to his congregation: 'Perhaps you are here to sit in judgement on my sermon – but at the Last Judgement you will have to answer for your part in it.' Michael Sadgrove comments,

It is a profound theological and pastoral insight to realise that the sermon is an event shaped in both the pulpit and the pew. This is true not simply of preaching but of every aspect of public ministry . . . Kierkegaard famously said that it is not the preacher who is the 'performer' but the hearer. The preacher is simply the prompter in the drama of human life as it is lived and performed before God. Ministry exists to 'prompt' that drama and coax human minds and hearts into life by pointing them to the hints, echoes and foresights of the kingdom of God, asking in effect 'do you see what I see?'[14]

The content of preaching

Jesus' first and continual message was 'the kingdom of heaven is at hand'.[15] He taught the disciples to pray for the coming of God's kingdom on earth as it is in heaven. All preaching is a variation on that theme, and in worship the Church anticipates the worship of the kingdom of heaven. Time is transcended as we preach from Scriptures that tell of God's saving actions in the past, interpret them for this congregation in this generation, and anticipate the time when 'the kingdom of this world has become the kingdom of our Lord and of his Messiah' (Revelation 11.15). Thus proclamation of the kingdom of heaven could be a faith-building and joyful glimpse of our future hope, or gentle and ultimately hopeful pastoral care for mourners at a funeral, a challenging call for ethical and compassionate living in the world or an invitation to turn to Christ for the first time in repentance and faith.

Most people come to church hoping to draw closer to God; they are not looking for advice, instruction or command so much as invitation and encouragement to risk more faithful and creative living as baptized Christians. 'We are looking and listening here for speech that will affirm and open the way to life, for speech that can be playful and not just useful, for words that disturb and change us not because they threaten but because they "fit" a reality we are just beginning to discern.'[16] When we take the preacher's words and run with them in our lives, we emerge from the sermon with the nerve to risk transformation. The fact that people bring their own interpretation to the preacher's words does not mean that the Church is automatically at the mercy of individual subjectivity. If people listen faithfully, their own unique response to our words will yet be orthodox because in Christ God shared our life so that we might share God's life: our response is caught up in our sharing God's life. Together preachers and hearers go on a journey with Christ and, like the disciples on the Emmaus road, emerge from the encounter not merely knowing more about their faith but about how to live it, having had an opportunity for transformation. Sangster's plea – that doctrines should be preached practically and duties doctrinally – sums it up: the kingdom of heaven is at hand, doctrine and praxis meet.

David Buttrick has expressed concern that the image of the kingdom of God has all but disappeared from contemporary preaching, erased by two World Wars, the Great Depression (we can add the various crises of the early twenty-first century) and the isolation of biblical history from human history leading to an emphasis in preaching on biblical history 'when, once upon a time, God was'. He believes that the Church has forgotten the excitement of God's unfolding future and therefore clings tenaciously to the past.[17] The antidote lies in Walter Brueggemann's eschatological perspective of preaching that 'does not describe a gospel-governed world but helps the congregation imagine it' and describes preaching as 'the chance to summon and nurture an alternative community with an alternative identity, vision and vocation, preoccupied with praise and obedient toward the God we Christians know fully in Jesus of Nazareth'.[18] All preaching has a fundamental element of hope as we hold out the vision of courage to live faithfully amid a torn world, in essence to help people find answers to that perplexed and anguished cry of the exiles in Babylon, 'How could we sing the LORD's song in a foreign land?' If people leave church more confident of the proximity of God's kingdom and better able to keep singing the Lord's song, we have preached faithfully. Rather than moralize we can enable people to grasp the impact of their baptism on their way of life and, while we don't tell people what to do, we help them to hear God speaking about decisions that they face. We can help them to ask themselves the questions that will eventually draw them closer to God; after all, the Christian life begins with penetrating questions at baptism and we need to go on being asked, and finding answers to, questions.

That takes us back to Nathan and his effective words to King David. It may come as a surprise to hear that this is a classic example of rhetorical skill in action. Whether he knew it or not (and he wouldn't have been able to name it as such, although it appears he knew very well what he was doing), Nathan used rhetoric to great effect, opening the way for God's message to be proclaimed and driven home. Put simply, rhetoric says a preacher should aim to attract (appeal to the mind), convert or turn (appeal to the will) and move or delight (appeal to the emotions) the hearers. This involves, more than the words we say, the way we say them, and it is the product of a lifetime: a performance of *Hamlet* by the Royal Shakespeare Company, whose actors have given their lives to the task, has a more powerful impact than an amateur performance in a village hall where goodwill only goes so far. While some fear, wrongly, that rhetoric stifles openness to the Holy Spirit's life-giving work, it remains a powerful conversation partner for preachers who through the years have sought the best ways to appeal, move and convert their hearers. Put simply, rhetoric discovers what needs to be said and describes how to say it most appropriately.[19] Congruence between what we say and how we say it, between our words and who we are, gives people confidence to listen and to trust that there is an integrity between preacher and sermon. Without that trust they will switch off. I will return to rhetoric later on; at this stage I merely note its contribution to preaching.

I have deliberately not attempted a definition of preaching but prefer to work with the idea of the wonder of preaching. Wonder is a response of awe, amazement or admiration in the face of something extraordinary and marvellous.[20] It reminds us that preaching emerges from encounter, encounter with God who is beyond our knowing and yet known in Jesus Christ and worshipped by the Church. Preaching is an attempt to give words to that wonder but it is always a trespass into mystery, so it is always provisional in human terms yet an expression of the gracious invitation of God who, since the beginning of creation, has been seeking human company. It is our privilege to be caught up in that wonder on behalf of other people.

Notes

1 *Common Worship, The Order of Priests, also called Presbyters.* Copyright © The Archbishops' Council 2005. Used by permission. Since I know the Anglican Church best, having been an active member since childhood principally in the UK but also in the USA, I draw from the Church of England when describing church life. I am not suggesting that this is normative for other churches, but it is easier to

interpret one church's specific practice in another context than it is to try to gain insights from a generic description of a combination of practices which ends up being not entirely true of any church. Members of other churches, who will find there is much common ground between churches, are asked to make their own extrapolations where necessary.

2 Thomas Long, *The Witness of Preaching*, Westminster John Knox, Louisville, 1989, p. 28.

3 Rowan Williams, 'The Sermon', in Stephen Conway (ed.), *Living the Eucharist: Affirming Catholicism and the Liturgy*, DLT, London, 2002, p. 46.

4 Rowan Williams, *Silence and Honey Cakes*, Lion, London, 2003, p. 66.

5 James Earl Massey, *Stewards of the Story: The Task of Preaching*, Westminster John Knox, Louisville, 2006, p. 3.

6 Calvin Miller, *The Sermon Maker: Tales of a Transformed Preacher*, Zondervan, Grand Rapids, 2002, p. 123.

7 That is not to discount things like *Thought for the Day* or *Pause for Thought* on the radio, but they are a different form of proclamation needing slightly different skills and methods which are not the focus of this book.

8 Lori Carrell, *The Great American Sermon Survey*, Mainstay Church Resources, Wheaton, IL, 2000, p. 95, quoted in Stephen Vincent De Leers, *Written Text becomes Living Word: The Vision and Practice of Sunday Preaching*, Liturgical Press, Collegeville, MN, 2004, p. 11.

9 This is normally reported as an instruction to preach with the Bible in one hand and the newspaper in the other, but Barth does not recall saying that. Princeton Seminary Center for Barth Studies quotes *Time* magazine, 31 May 1963, as the nearest to the assumed quotation. See http://libweb.ptsem/edu/collections/barth/faq/quotes/aspz?menu=296&subText=468.

10 Timothy Radcliffe, *Why Go to Church?* Continuum, London, 2008 p. 41, quoting Augustine, *De catechizandis rubibus* 2.4.

11 Michael Monshau, 'A Catholic Conversation about Preaching', in Michael Monshau (ed.), *Preaching at the Double Feast: Homiletics for Eucharistic Worship*, Liturgical Press, Collegeville, MN, 2006, pp. 24–5.

12 Gail Ramshaw, *Worship: Searching for Language*, Pastoral Press, Portland, OR, 1988, p. 155.

13 DeLeers, *Written Text becomes Living Word*, pp. 49, 50.

14 Michael Sadgrove, *Wisdom and Ministry*, SPCK, London, 2008, p. 12.

15 See, for example, Mark 1.15 and Mark 14.25 and their equivalents in the other Gospels: from first to last he proclaimed the kingdom of God.

16 Williams, *Silence and Honey Cakes*, p. 71.

17 David Buttrick, *Preaching the New and the Now*, Westminster John Knox, Louisville, 1998, back cover, pp. 1–2.

18 Walter Brueggemann, *The Word Militant: Preaching a Decentering Word*, Fortress Press, Minneapolis, 2007, pp. 27, 56.

19 Thomas A. Sloane (ed.), *Dictionary of Rhetoric*, Oxford University Press, 2001, is an invaluable and fascinating resource.

20 Derived from the definitions in *The Chambers Dictionary*, Chambers Harrap, Edinburgh, 1998.

2

THE CHURCH'S PREACHING
IN THE PAST

I have already referred to the resource that rhetoric offers to the Church in its preaching and, before we begin a review of the preaching inheritance from the past, some understanding of rhetoric is necessary because it will crop up again and again. Aristotle (*c*.384–322BC) was the father of rhetoric and defined it as 'the faculty of discovering in the particular case what are the available means of persuasion'. He thought that training enabled some people to speak and move an audience more effectively than others. This is not just technique but involves the speaker's character and knowledge of the hearers. Classical public speaking divides every persuasive speech into four structural parts,

> The *exodium* states the subject and catches people's attention – in a sermon this is the introduction;
> the *narration* explains the situation and gives necessary background – this is largely the discussion of the biblical or theological material;
> the *proof* outlines what action should follow from the material presented so far – this is the description of how to turn doctrine into practice, how to live the gospel;
> the *peroration* is the recapitulation aimed to kindle emotion and response – this is the conclusion which should inspire people to do something about what they have heard.

Cicero (c.106–43BC) developed and refined Aristotle's ideas, saying that the function of rhetoric was to persuade an audience to respond to truth that had been discovered by reason. Note the truth part of the equation: rhetoric is not just an appeal to the emotions but is rooted in truth, and preachers must be theologians who can speak truth about God. Cicero systematized Aristotle's ideas into five principles: essentially a speaker discovers what should be said (invention), arranges the speech in a particular order based on purposeful intention (arrangement), clothes the thoughts with language (style), secures the speech (memory) and delivers the speech effectively.

Early Christian preachers like Chrysostom and Augustine were trained rhetoricians, and through the centuries preachers have used rhetorical principles even though their expression has varied. The original oral-based rhetoric of the Greeks and Romans was reworked in the written-language-based rhetoric of the post-Reformation period and re-evaluated again in the eighteenth century when the Enlightenment introduced new disciplines like science and challenged some traditional beliefs and understandings. In the late twentieth century there was further rethinking to accommodate the impact of television and film, then the electronic revolution. This has led to new questions about how art and architecture, dance and music might be used to rhetorical effect and the realization that preachers (like English teachers) can no longer rely on their hearers to know Scripture or to recognize quotations from the Bible. In an age of short soundbites people are not used to listening to prolonged speech in the way that they once did but are bombarded in everyday life with concrete sensory images. As forAristotle in his day, the challenge is to discover the available means of persuasion in our day and how best to use them. Barack Obama has been described as the greatest orator of his generation: his campaign speeches were masterpieces of rhetorical skill in their construction, scripting and delivery, leading experts to say that his delivery is as important as his words,[1] although he describes his natural style as rambling, hesitant and overly verbose.[2]

To know how to move forward in preaching, it helps if we can inhabit and know our inherited tradition, otherwise we cannot decide whether to learn from its wisdom or, unnecessarily, repeat its mistakes. So we turn to a brief review of some aspects of that tradition which is inevitably selective, glosses or omits significant parts of this history and misses some of the great names of preaching, but is intended to set a context for the future rather than be definitive of the past.

The early centuries

From the start, preaching in the context of worship had a dual focus of instruction and exhortation: Justin Martyr referred in his *Apologies* to the second-century Christians gathering for worship, where they heard the memoirs of the apostles (the Gospels) or the writings of the prophets followed by the president instructing and exhorting them to imitate these good things.[3] In the early centuries the bishop explained the Scriptures as part of the Eucharist, and in several places there was also a daily preaching ministry, particularly after Easter when the newly baptized were instructed in the faith they had embraced. Preachers explained the Scriptures literally or allegorically and applied them to the hearers. In the fourth century John Chrysostom, probably the greatest preacher of this period, insisted on disciplined and arduous study, prayer and abandonment to the Holy Spirit and the spontaneous promptings of our thoughts.[4] He also argued that since pagans were attacking Christianity using rhetorical skills, the Church should use them to counter the attacks and, in pastoral preaching, to address the difficulties facing the people. His sermons, like his character, have been described as 'outspoken and direct'[5] and were the expression of his rhetorical training which he adapted when explaining the biblical texts. Also in the fourth century, Gregory of Nazianzus considered that the purpose of pastoral ministry included watching over and making Christ dwell by the Spirit in the heart of the baptized and guiding them through their ongoing transformation (divinization). With these aims in mind, the first of the bishop's duties was the administration of the word, which he did through preaching, teaching, counselling and celebrating the mysteries (the Eucharist). Word and sacrament were inseparable, and the preacher was to proclaim the word, regulate the truth of his own opinions with judgement and take care not to preach heresy. Preaching thus had a didactic and formational purpose, and in his final, moving oration at the Council of Constantinople in 381, Gregory spoke of the outcome of his teaching as a people who were united to one another and to God by unity in trinitarian doctrine.[6]

Augustine was steeped in the rhetorical tradition, which he taught for many years. Following his conversion, he recognized that Cicero's categories of style could be correlated with the different literary styles of the Bible. He wrote the earliest homiletics textbook, *On Christian Doctrine*, Book 4 of which is devoted to homiletics and oratory and contains a justification for the use of rhetorical techniques appropriate to the occasion. These should be combined with wisdom, and the Church should beware the person who speaks eloquent nonsense: just because it sounds eloquent does not make it true. The preacher must choose words carefully to ensure they are understood. He quoted, with approval, Cicero's dictum that the speaker aims to teach, to delight and to move, stressing that while teaching was the greatest, preachers should aim to sway the mind and subdue the will and should choose words appropriate for the task rather than to draw attention to themselves.[7]

The Council of Cloveshoo, 747, mandated priests to exercise diligence in instilling the creed into people so they knew what to believe and hope for. At this time the emphasis was on teaching rather than preaching. Charlemagne called for weekly vernacular sermons in all parish churches, which were often verse-by-verse comment on a biblical passage, but later many parish clergy read from collections of homilies from the Fathers. It was not until the thirteenth century that the new preaching orders shifted the emphasis to preaching rather than teaching and promoted sermons structured like a tree with a trunk (the theme), subdivisions into boughs (clauses), and further subdivisions into branches (sub-clauses). Long and complex sermons could result, leading Thomas Waleys, of the University of Oxford, to give practical advise to fourteenth-century preachers not to weary hearers by prolixity but to stop before they become restive.[8] He advocated intelligible and attractive delivery, not odiously noisy or indistinct, and gives an interesting vignette about 'preachers who seemed to be engaged in a sort of all-in wrestling bout, hurling themselves about with such violence that they would have pushed the pulpit over if people had not rushed to hold it up'.[9] Charles Smyth's critique is that while this preaching was clever and ingenious, 'its connection with the Word of God though undeniable, is purely superficial and purely formal. There is no wrestling here with the Word, no preaching as of a dying man to dying men. The text from Scripture is supposed to be the preacher's theme, it is in fact merely the peg on which he hangs an academic exercise.'[10]

The Reformation

The Reformation shifted the context of preaching from adversarial scholastic assemblies to lively gatherings of ordinary people. Liturgical reforms meant that preaching was less a preparation for receiving the sacrament and more a way of imparting the word of God. Erasmus emphasized teaching through sermons while Luther thought that the word of God has three manifestations, the incarnate word, the written word, and the proclaimed word. Preaching was the medium of salvation, the proclamation of the gospel for people to hear and appropriate through faith. His style was popular, often conversational, and influenced by rhetorical training. Calvin disagreed with Luther and believed that preaching was the word of God only insofar as it expounded and interpreted the Bible; it took the ratification of the Holy Spirit to make a sermon the revealed word of God. Calvin normally preached extemporaneously; having reminded his hearers of the previous sermon, he exegeted each section of the Scripture in turn, reconstructing the original meaning and applying it to the life of the congregation, exhorting them to obedience. Zwingli centred worship on the sermon rather than the Eucharist and favoured course preaching through books of the Bible.

A Bible was placed in every church in England and clergy who were not licensed to preach read lengthy homilies expounding the Reformed faith from the two Books of Homilies (1547 and 1571).[11] Among the preachers, Hugh Latimer was influenced by Erasmus and Luther and preached colloquially, avoiding subdivisions and without an outline beyond that offered by his text. Woodcuts show people listening to a sermon with open Bibles, and the effectiveness of preaching is shown by martyrs under Mary who, within four years of the 1552 Prayer Book's denial of transubstantiation, could counter their interrogators using Scripture.[12]

Homilies drew criticism for being generic and not prepared for particular congregations. Archbishop Edmund Grindal noted that 'The godly preacher . . . can apply his speech according to the diversity of times, places and hearers, which cannot be done in homilies: exhortation, reprehension and persuasions are uttered with more affection, to the moving of hearers, in sermon than homilies.'[13] Following Elizabeth's accession, theologians and preachers returned with Calvin's ideals for preaching and there was increasing division between the Puritans, who insisted on exposition from the pulpit, and those who believed that Scripture could speak for itself. The Puritan influence led to 'prophesyings' springing up around the country. These were popular weekly gatherings where ministers read the text, helped people to understand it and summarized useful points of doctrine which were applied 'to the manners of men in a simple and plain speech'.[14] The numerous divisions and subdivisions of the text, explorations and discussions could take hours. In 1570, the Bishop of Chichester trained 40 preachers to accompany him to the main towns of his diocese, but the Queen disapproved and Archbishop Grindal argued with her that 'where preaching wanteth, obedience faileth'.[15]

There were fewer licensed preachers than parishes at the turn of the seventeenth century,[16] but some preachers drew crowds. Lancelot Andrewes was steeped in the Scriptures and used rhetorical methods to bring out the meaning of words. Emphasizing the relationship of prayer and preaching, he described priests as 'the Lord's remembrancers bringing the people to God in prayer, both private and public, and God before them in preaching'. Ellen Davis observes of him, 'To look again and again at the words of scripture, with fascination and confidence that there is something we have not yet heard – that is the most important hermeneutical practice Andrewes learned from the Fathers and the one we may also learn from him.'[17] John Donne drew large crowds to St Paul's Cathedral and saw the role of preaching as to convey Christ, to bring heaven and earth to each other. His sermons emphasized application to life and he said that he searched Scriptures not as a concordance but as a wardrobe, not to make an inventory but to find something to wear; his sermons have been described as 'not so much a reasoned exposition of the text as a recollected one'.[18] Rather than giving an exposition, Donne dissected two or three verses and brought other Scriptures to bear on them. In contrast – and anticipating new approaches to preaching – George Herbert thought Donne 'crumbled the text' and treated it as a dictionary. He preferred to take longer portions of Scripture in sermons (of no longer than an hour – a limit enforced in the 1630s, along with a ban on controversial topics[19]) which addressed the congregation's needs using easily remembered stories to help them in their lives.[20] Faced with 'thick and heavy' people, he preached from 'moving and ravishing' texts, hoping to transport and enchant his people rather than entertain or inform them.[21] From the Puritan tradition, Richard Baxter's advice was that 'all our teaching must be as plain and evident as we can make it . . . He that would be understood must speak to the capacity of his hearers and make it his business to make himself understood.'[22] However, this was no excuse for not stretching the people, 'See that you preach . . . some higher points, that stall their understandings and feed them not with all milk, but sometimes with stronger meat.'[23]

The Restoration and beyond

The relationship of word and sacrament changed with the Reformation to the extent that in some places, especially during the Commonwealth period, the rest of the service was merely the support act for the sermon. In contrast, in the Roman Catholic Church the celebrant could omit a sermon altogether.[24] With the restoration of liturgical worship in 1662, the Church of England required a sermon at Holy Communion, thus allowing word and sacrament to create together the context for God to meet and transform the Church. In practice communion was infrequent and sermons were normally preached at Morning and Evening Prayer (where they were not mandated), thus challenging preachers to achieve through the word what the absence of the sacrament left undone.

Charles II liked the extempore style he heard during his exile, and on his return unsuccessfully commanded preachers at Cambridge University to deliver their sermons in Latin and English from memory without books, the names of those who failed to do so being reported to him. But preaching was changing and John Evelyn caught the mood of the transition in his 1683 diary entry, 'A stranger, and old man, preach'd on 6 Jerem. V 8 . . . much after Bp Andrews's method, full of logical divisions, in short and broken periods, and Latin sentences, now quite out of fashion in the pulpit, which is grown into a far more profitable way, of plain and practical discourses.'[25] In 1661, Jeremy Taylor, the Bishop of Down and Connor, exhorted his clergy, 'Do not spend your Sermons in general and indefinite things, as in Exhortations to the people to get Christ, to be united to Christ, and things of the like unlimited signification; but tell them in every duty what are the measures, what circumstances, what instrument, and what is the particular minute meaning of every general Advice.'[26] The aim of the sermon was 'to make men good, not to intoxicate their brains with notions, or to furnish their heads with a systeme of opinions; but to reform men's lives and purifie their natures'.[27]

John Tillotson, Archbishop of Canterbury from 1691 to 1694, exemplified the move towards simplicity in sermons which nevertheless retained rhetorical underpinnings. He used short and clear sentences in a sermon in which 'the whole Thread was of a piece, plain and distinct. No affectation of Learning, no squeezing of Texts, no superficial Strains, no false thoughts nor bold flights, all was solid and yet lively, and grave as well as fine.'[28] The pendulum swung so far that sermons became sober exhortations to live upright lives rather than the proclamation of the kingdom of God, and in 1724 the Bishop of London had to remind his clergy that they were 'Christian Preachers, not barely preachers of Morality'.[29]

In the eighteenth century lay people wanted scholarly sermons, and many preachers used books of sermons since few had much theological training. Latitudinarian preachers aimed to reform lives through impersonal, objective preaching, unlike the Methodists, who were intensely personal and preached for conversion, often in the open air. Much could be said about the creative influence of Methodism on preaching; evangelistic preaching often began in the classical style but, after the exposition of the text, made a personal appeal aiming for conviction of sin and repentance. John Wesley's sermons look very doctrinal on paper but led critics to denounce his ugly enthusiasm, something that evoked the desired response from his hearers whom he addressed directly in the second person; while George Whitefield's preaching moved people, although later many could not remember what he had said: it was preaching for the moment and the response at the time was what mattered. The liveliness of their sermons contrasted with the dullness of those in the established church, as Hogarth's prints illustrate vividly.

The nineteenth and twentieth centuries

A middle way emerged between rational and emotional preaching. An Oxford don, Richard Whatley, advocated didactic preaching to defend the faith against challenges, for example from science, in which the preacher started from a widely supported proposition and argued it so that the onus was on those who disagreed with it. Books gave outlines of the essential doctrines and ideas for how to preach them using the normal method of subdivision of the subject, the discussion of propositions and then a reminder of the opening proposition which had now been proven. The destination of the sermon was never in doubt, only the route taken to reach it. Whatley influenced both John Henry Newman and Frederick Robertson, who took preaching towards Romanticism, although Newman never followed Whatley fully but preferred to open up discussion between two extreme positions on any subject. Newman thought that preachers should eliminate anything that distracted from the spiritual good of the hearers and preparation involved assimilating that goal so that he could preach with earnestness, addressing their situation and getting them to use their imagination as a way of persuading them. He used manuscripts in his university sermons but later, once a Roman Catholic, abandoned them and was said to be rambling and dreary, often unprepared and prone to wreck the balance of sentences by his choice of words.[30]

Robertson was one of the giants of nineteenth-century Anglican preaching, although in his time little known outside Brighton, where he preached for six years until his early death in 1853. Intense, sickly, sensitive and a lover of poetry and nature, he had perceptive insight. In preaching he aimed to establish positive truth rather than destroy error, addressed social problems and new scientific challenges, and understood that faith was sometimes hard for his hearers. He began from a personal or spiritual problem and made a biblical character who suffered from it the focus of his sermon. Bishop Hensley Henson wrote, '[Robertson's] power as a preacher derived from three sources: first his exact and extensive knowledge of the Bible, second the deliberate reference of his preaching to modern conditions of thought and life, and the intensely personal note which runs through it, and lastly and principally, the passionate devotion to the Person of the Lord Jesus Christ which inspires all his words.'[31]

Charles Simeon drew large congregations to Holy Trinity Church, Cambridge, and gave lessons in sermon composition to would-be preachers. As a nineteenth-century evangelical, his primary focus was on the cross and he preached for conversion and commitment. Inspired by Jean Claude, a French Huguenot, he revived the medieval formal scheme of sermon composition, in which the sermon was based on a carefully chosen text but was not simply textual exegesis so much as an exposition of biblical theology: it was to be clear, give the sense of the whole text (not just a phrase within it), bring comfort and excite acts of practical piety. It should not tell all the preacher knew but what the people could receive.[32]

From a very different (Southern Baptist) tradition, John Broadus[33] favoured neither rational nor emotional preaching but the use of the imagination and, like Newman and Robertson, put romantic preaching in the mainstream.[34] He emphasized the moral character of the preacher and his devotion to God, along with clear thinking, and knowledge of religious truth and of human nature, all accompanied by skill in style, delivery, and the collection, choice and arrangement of material. He advocated preaching the great doctrines of the faith without lecturing, perhaps adopting a different point of view or making connections between the doctrine and the daily life of the hearers. Morality should only be preached with reference to the atonement and the work of the Spirit; historical sermons should be about people since biblical history is really biography and all preaching should evoke both intellectual interest and action.[35]

The Oxford Movement helped to redress any over-emphasis on the word at the expense of sacrament: the sermon was not the focus but a part of the whole experience of worship that drew people to a sense of the holiness of God through symbols, ceremonies, ritual, music, colour and architecture. These preachers aimed less at intellectual understanding and more at encounter with the mystery of God. From within this tradition, Paul Bull's 1922 book on preaching kept the schematic approach to sermon construction and Jesus' example of preaching that the kingdom of God is at hand but cautioned against preaching the kingdom and ignoring the king.[36] For Bull, the priest's duties in preaching were to instruct the people in the doctrines of the faith and in the manner of life they involve, stimulate a hunger and thirst for righteousness and help them to think God's thoughts.[37] In contrast, in the USA there were moves towards preaching as pastoral counselling.

The great twentieth-century Methodist preacher W. E. Sangster quoted as a maxim that 'doctrines must be preached practically and duties doctrinally' and challenged preachers to be both exhorters and teachers using four approaches to preaching: the authoritative, the persuasive, the co-operative ('let's look at this perplexing matter together') and the subversive (assuming an intellectual position the preacher does not hold and arguing for it before demolishing it). He noted the dangers of abdicating the choice of themes to the caprice of public taste rather than the Holy Spirit and of merely making moral comment on contemporary events so that the pulpit ceased to be the throne of the word of God. The preacher should make topical references in order to be relevant but should not be driven by what was in the press.[38]

Like all his predecessors, he followed the traditional rhetorical approach to preaching and identified five main forms of the sermon: exposition, argument, faceting, categorizing, analogy, saying that preachers should vary their approach to keep congregations on their toes. He warned against undue complexity or forcing sermon divisions to be alliterative – I remember one preacher who had clearly never read that advice and regularly had six or seven alliterative subdivisions! Expository sermons should explain the text but the preacher should avoid disempowering the congregation by constantly telling them 'what it really means', thus implying that reading the Bible required specialized training. In argument sermons the theme was announced and then argued in a clear progression of thought, with either universal principles or a specific reality or dilemma.[39] In a faceting sermon Sangster cut to a pattern as one would a jewel, turning the truth in the light of God. In categorizing sermons Sangster broke the content into various categories and applied it to different groups of people (the young, the elderly), or to different parts of human nature (Sangster suggested reason, ambition, conscience) or to different periods of time (the past, the future and the present). Finally there were analogy sermons (the Church as a body) but Sangster warned against pressing things too far (are you the tonsils? – we are no worse off when you are gone – or are you the appendix? – we didn't know we had you until you caused us trouble!).

The biblical theology movement of the first half of the twentieth century embodied developments in biblical studies and stressed expository preaching that led people to encounter with God. To take one example, the theologian Karl Barth's regular sermons to prisoners were pervaded by theological thinking but very simple in presentation. He used repetition to aid understanding and recollection, reading some words of Scripture and speaking on them, then repeating the same words while adding another phrase before speaking to that, until he had expounded the whole Scripture passage. Given the prison context, his message was upbeat and his aim was that the prisoners should know themselves loved by God.[40]

Writing from the Baptist tradition, R. E. O. White favoured exegetical preaching and drew from the classical rhetorical tradition. The sermon should take a religious truth, justify it from Scripture, clarify it, illustrate it, make it memorable and apply it persuasively to the listeners; the final test of a sermon was what it made people do.[41] Preaching should set people among the big truths, the towering ideals and the bedrock convictions of the faith that lend new perspective to daily life.[42] Martin Lloyd Jones's 30 years in the pulpit of Westminster

Chapel, London, made that church a centre for expository preaching that began with explanation of the text but then led to discussion of the biblical doctrine thus revealed and its application to the hearers. In advocating this approach, he opposed what he called 'commentary' preaching and topical preaching. He would not be bound by time limits because he believed they constrained the Spirit's work and defined preaching as 'logic on fire', believing that preaching needed to be the logical demonstration of biblical truth but open to the Spirit's fire. In retirement he edited many volumes of his sermons.

This inevitably incomplete overview of preaching highlights a basic methodology and reliance on rhetorical principles which ran through all the changes in style: preachers began either from a text or from a theme and constructed (the word is significant) a sermon with a recognized, often complex, framework. The emphasis shifted in different periods, but there was normally an element of teaching and an element of preaching for response, whether that was expressed in a moral life or evangelical conversion. Preachers tried to make the sermon relevant and interesting but there was never any real questioning of the overall approach, which is why the revolution in preaching that began in the 1970s was so radical. Just as the dawn of the age of print, combined with the ecclesial and theological shifts of the Reformation, led to the then new emphasis on the exegesis and application of Scripture to people's lives, so the dawn of the age of electronic communication, combined with the developments in biblical hermeneutics and theological perspectives, opened up new possibilities. At the same time, in the Roman Catholic Church, the Second Vatican Council set in motion very substantial changes in preaching, giving it new emphasis by affirming in 1967 that,

> The preaching of the word is necessary for the administration of the sacraments. For the sacraments are sacraments of faith and faith has its origin in the word . . . in this way the Church feeds upon the bread of life as it comes from the table of both the word of God and the body of Christ . . . In

the readings, explained by the homily, God is speaking to his people, opening up to them the mystery of redemption and salvation, and nourishing their spirit; Christ is present to the faithful through his own word. The homily is an integral part of the liturgy and . . . it is necessary for the nurturing of the Christian life. It should develop some point of the readings . . . and take into account the mystery being celebrated and the needs proper to the listeners.[43]

The homily is to be an act of proclamation of the wonderful works of God, not just explanation, and is to be seen as part of the liturgy. It is less about arguments and elegant style than it is speaking 'in a way that is filled with faith, redolent of the sacred scriptures and expressive of pastoral love'.[44] Those sentiments were equally those of the other churches as they explored new preaching territory in the 1970s.

Notes

1 One British speech-writer described Obama's style of delivery as 'basically churchy – it's religious: the way he slides down some words and hits others – the intonation, the emphasis, the pauses and the silences. He is close to singing, just as preaching is close to singing. All writing is a rhythm of kinds and he brings it out, hits the tune. It's about the tune, not the lyrics, with Obama.' Philip Collins, in Stephanie Holmes, *Obama: Oratory and Originality*, http://news.bbc.co.uk/1/hi/world/americas/7735014.stm, accessed 19 November 2008. The report has some significant observations about rhetorical style and includes an extract from Obama's victory speech.

2 Barack Obama, *The Audacity of Hope*, Canongate, Edinburgh, 2007, p. 120.

3 Justin Martyr, *First Apology* 67.

4 John Chrysostom, *On the Priesthood*, in particular Book 5, which addresses aspects of preaching.

5 Henry Chadwick, *The Early Church*, Penguin Books, Harmondsworth, 1967, p. 186.

6 Gregory of Nazianzus, *Oration* 2.22, 35, 36; 42.15.

7 Augustine, *On Christian Doctrine* 4.3, 7, 24, 27–31, 38.

8 Thomas Waleys, *De Modo Componendi Sermones cum Docu-*

*mentis, c.*1340, quoted in Charles Smyth, *The Art of Preaching: a Practical Survey of Preaching in the Church of England 747–1939*, SPCK, London, 1940, 1953, p. 37.

9 Smyth, *Art of Preaching*, pp. 35 and 37.

10 Smyth, *Art of Preaching*, p. 53.

11 From 1548 until 1642, preachers required a licence if they were to preach. Essentially this gave the state control over what was said in the pulpit in turbulent times but also addressed the problem of clergy who were not trained to preach in the new environment of the Reformation.

12 See *Foxe's Book of Martyrs* for examples, although it is important to bear in mind that Foxe was essentially writing propaganda for the Protestant cause.

13 Philip E. Hughes, *Theology of the English Reformers*, Hodder, London, 1965.

14 William Perkins, *The Arte of Prophesying* (Latin 1592, English 1607). The records of the trials of martyrs during the reign of Queen Mary indicate the remarkable extent to which lay people, both men and women, were able to defend their beliefs by reference to Scripture.

15 A. G. Dickens, *The English Reformation*, Pennsylvania State University Press, 2nd edn, 1989, p. 373.

16 Roy Strong quotes a figure of 920 licensed preachers in 1,255 parishes in 1603. Roy Strong, *A Little History of the English Country Church*, Jonathan Cape, London, 2007, p. 137.

17 Ellen Davis, *Wondrous Depth: Preaching the Old Testament*, Westminster John Knox, Louisville, 2005, p. 102.

18 Davis, *Wondrous Depth*, pp. 75, 79.

19 Strong, *Little History*, p. 137.

20 George Herbert, *The Complete English Poems*, ed. John Tobin, Penguin Books, London, 1991, pp. 295, 209.

21 Herbert, *Complete English Poems*, p. 209.

22 Richard Baxter, *The Reformed Pastor*, Epworth Press, London, 1939, pp. 136–7.

23 Baxter, *Reformed Pastor*, p. 151.

24 Michael Monshau, 'A Catholic Conversation about Preaching', in Michael Monshau (ed.), *Preaching at the Double Feast: Homiletics for Eucharistic Worship*, Liturgical Press, Collegeville, MN, 2006, p. 1.

25 John Evelyn, *Diary and Correspondence of John Evelyn, Esq., F.R.S.*, ed. William Bray; new edn H. B. Wheatley, 1906, vol. ii, p. 412.

26 Jeremy Taylor, *Rules and Advices to the Clergy of the Diocese of Down and Connor for their Deportment in their Personal and Publick Capacities 1661*, in John R. H. Moorman (ed.), *The Curate of Souls: Being a Collection of Writings on the Nature and Work of a Priest from*

the First Century after the Restoration 1660–1760, SPCK, London, 1958.

27 Edward Fowler, *The Principles and Practice of Certain Moderate Divines . . . 1670*, quoted in Smyth, *Art of Preaching*, p. 168.

28 Bishop Gilbert Burnet, quoted in W. F. Mitchell, *English Pulpit Oratory from Andrewes to Tillotson*, SPCK, London, 1932, 1962, pp. 334–5.

29 Edward Gibson, *Directions given to the Clergy in the Diocese of London in the Year 1724 by the Right Reverend Father in God, Edmund, Lord Bishop of London*, 2nd edn 1727, p. 19.

30 A. W. Hutton in his personal remembrances of Cardinal Newman described his preaching as 'rambling and dreary . . . I often used to lament that he did not write out and read something which might have been half the length and yet a thousand times more effective; and while I think that his attempts at spoken sermons were partly due to an idea that preaching ought not to be reading, I am bound to add that I believe indolence and a sort of contempt for the congregation he had to address were partly responsible for them . . . Newman was, even in his Anglican days, essentially a writer for the pulpit rather than a great preacher. If you read Newman aloud you will discover that he continually wrecks the balance of the sentence, often by quite trivial blunders, such as employing a dactyl in place of a spondee, or vice versa' (A. W. Hutton, *The Expositor*, 4th Series, 2 (1890), pp. 238, 224). It is open to question whether most preachers today would know a dactyl or a spondee if they saw one in their sermon, but it is the difference between saying 'The Holy Comforter' (dactyl) and 'The Holy Spirit' (spondee): a dactyl has the stress 'Oom-pa-pa', with the emphasis on the first syllable, while a spondee has the equal stress 'boom-boom'.

31 Hensley Henson, *Robertson of Brighton 1816–1853*, Smith Elder, London, 1916, pp. 91–2.

32 Jean Claude, *Traité de la Composition d'un Sermon (An essay on the composition of a sermon)*, trans. Robert Robinson, 1779. Quoted in Smyth, *Art of Preaching*, pp. 185ff.

33 John Broadus, *On the Preaching and Delivery of Sermons*, London 1870; new rev. edn by Jesse Burton Weatherspoon, Harper Brothers, New York, 1944, pp. 6–7.

34 O. C. Edwards, *A History of Preaching*, Abingdon Press, Nashville, 2004, p. 657.

35 Broadus, *On the Preaching and Delivery of Sermons*, pp. 60–84.

36 Paul Bull, *Lectures on Preaching and Sermon Construction*, SPCK, London, 1922, p. 62.

37 Bull, *Lectures*, p. 186.

38 Bull, *Lectures*, pp. 48–9.

39 Bull, *Lectures*, pp. 59–110.

40 See Karl Barth, *Deliverance to the Captives*, SCM Press, London, 1961, which contains many sermons preached in Basel prison.

41 R. E. O. White, *A Guide to Preaching*, Pickering and Inglis, London, 1973, pp. 40–2, 79.

42 White, *Guide to Preaching*, pp. 89, 13–15.

43 Sacred Congregation for the Rites (Consilium), Instruction on the Worship of the Eucharist (*Eucharisticum Mysterium*) 9, in *Documents on the Liturgy* 179, 20, 41, quoted in *Written Text becomes Living Word: The Vision and Practice of Sunday Preaching*, Liturgical Press, Collegeville, MN, 2004, pp. 17–19.

44 Sacred Congregation for the Rites, *Eucharisticum Mysterium*, quoted on pp. 26–7.

3

PREACHING TRANSFORMED

The New Homiletic

Amid the social and cultural upheavals of the 1960s, the Church clung to traditional deductive approaches. With the 1970s dawned the homiletic revolution which accompanied the electronic era in communication and is now seen to be as significant as the transformation of preaching by the printing press. The roots of the Reformation's word-based, literary culture had been the growing influence of Greek culture, with its different alphabet and thought processes from the more oral Semitic culture. It came into its own with printing and the shift from the ear to the eye, a world where seeing rather than hearing is believing. Oratory based on the written word is propositional: people think in ideas developed as rational argument. Literary sermons are tightly knit and closely reasoned expositions of theological doctrine with clear and logical arguments, development of key points and persuasive reasoning.[1] However, preaching is an oral form of communication and in the 1970s the Church began to recover that foundation.

The essential transformation was from deductive preaching to inductive preaching, the term 'inductive' being used, as in scientific enquiry, to describe the movement from particular experience to general conclusion, in contrast to the deductive move from the general to the specific.[2] The sermon becomes not a tightly structured thesis presented to a passive congregation, but a shared journey led by the preacher with the congregation as active participants who develop their own insights as the sermon progresses. Theologically the locus of authority shifts from the preacher to the whole church, as preacher and congregation interact together with the biblical text. To avoid the text becoming secondary to the experience of the hearers, leading to individualism in interpretation, the preacher has a responsibility to inhabit and interpret the larger theological tradition for and with the congregation.

The first preachers to enter the debate on the new homiletic tended to agree more on the identification of the issues than on ways to address them. Fred Craddock, from the Disciples of Christ tradition (which, significantly for his thesis, stresses the priesthood of all believers), maintained a commitment to serious biblical scholarship and to preaching, despite the authority of both being challenged by the culture of the 1960s. In his 1971 book, *As One Without Authority*, he tried to take account of the changes insofar as they affected preaching methodology. His focus on the role of the hearers raises important questions of language and communication as well as the form of the sermon. Craddock wants to help preachers bring the excitement of insights gleaned during their own study of Scripture into the pulpit, and he describes the impasse:

The preacher cannot recapture his former enthusiasm [for discoveries made during the process of exegesis] as he breaks his theme into points, unless, of course, his image of himself is that of one who passes the truth from the summit down to the people. The brief temptation to re-create in the pulpit his own process of discovering is warded off by the clear recollection of seminary warnings that the minister does not take his desk into the pulpit. What, then, is he to do? If he is a good preacher, he refuses to be dull. And so between the three or four 'points' that mark the dull deductive trail he plants humour, anecdotes, illustrations, poetry or perhaps enlivening hints of heresy and threats of butchering sacred cows. But the perceptive preacher knows instinctively that something is wrong with his sermon: not its exegetical support, not its careful preparation, not its relevance; it is the movement that is wrong.[3]

Craddock's answer is to turn the traditional approach on its head and, instead of announcing his conclusion first and then proving it, he takes his hearers on a journey towards a previously unrevealed conclusion. The sermon becomes an event, a voyage of discovery or pilgrimage, where preacher and congregation explore together and the preacher is the catalyst for everyone's participation. The sermon the preacher has on paper is not the last word that people will take away because the congregation's responsibility is to work at listening to and engaging with the sermon, bringing their own thoughts and interpretations to what is said. It becomes liturgy, the work of the people, in the truest sense of the word.

Being a biblical scholar, Craddock's preaching centres on the biblical text but he avoids mere exegesis and does not support topical preaching. As befits the ecclesiology of the Disciples of Christ, he honours the vocation of all Christians to study Scripture for themselves and to reach their own conclusions and believes that if people are helped to unearth their own insights they will remember them. He encouraged his students to explore the various forms of Scripture, allowing them to shape sermons which, as Augustine had advocated, respected the integrity of the original text. Thus a sermon on Scripture that expresses the praise of the people should lead the contemporary congregation to praise.[4] Craddock draws on rhetorical insights and communication methodology to produce very focused, concrete, often anecdotal, sermons that begin from particulars and concrete life experience because he believes people can draw general conclusions as the preacher helps them towards their own *eureka* moment.

In a later book, Craddock proposes that preaching must include the content of the faith if it is not to be empty intensity and hollow exhortation. Preaching is 'both words and the Word'.[5] Biblical texts have a future as well as a past and preaching continues the conversation into the present, making the Scriptures a living voice in the congregation. He advocates the recovery of rhetorical practice and training in speech communication for preachers, that the person of the preacher is a vital element in effective preaching, that the congregation are active participants and need to be given time and encouragement to engage with the sermon as it was preached, rather than just to 'go and do' afterwards.[6]

This revolutionary approach dislodged the log that was causing the log jam and others soon joined the conversation about preaching methodology. The literature today is vast and comes from a variety of traditions including the African-American tradition and an emerging literature about women's preaching.[7]

David Buttrick's 1987 book, *Homiletic: Moves and Structures*,[8] focuses on rhetorical strategies in sermon construction. Critical of both the biblical theology view that God is 'out there' and the therapeutic view that God is 'in here', he argues for a new partnership of preaching and rhetoric to facilitate the formation of secure Christian identity in the Church and individuals. He highlights the importance of language as preachers use images and patterns in the sermon to build a 'faith world' in which the hearer can live with integrity. He is best-known for his proposal that a sermon should contain five or six 'moves' or sections. Preachers are like photographers' assistants, setting up scenes and encouraging the congregation to take mental photographs of them. The preacher's task is to construct a sermon that leaves people not with random photographs but with a clearly linked sequence, like a filmstrip, so they can remember and interpret each photo in the context of the whole sermon.

The preacher is in charge of the focus of each move within the sermon. Buttrick thought that four minutes is the longest attention span people can give to a single idea or 'move' and that during that time there must be a beginning, a middle and an end. The beginning states the main idea and links it back to the previous move; the middle develops, clarifies or illustrates it, perhaps identifying problems, and the brief conclusion brings closure, readying people for the next move. At each stage the aim is to get hearers to take a mental photograph. Christian rhetoric puts Christian understandings together with lived experience, and preaching involves a 'bringing out' or a 'bringing into view' of beliefs about God, God's purposes and grace in human lives through a variety of rhetorical means: depiction, analogy, metaphor, explanation, analysis and creedal exploration. Buttrick argues against preaching as trading in formal proofs which make reason rather than faith decisive. Christian preaching draws a clear line between Christian understandings and common social attitudes, speaking tenderly but critically of the latter – the gospel's anticipation of reconciled peace on earth is not jingoism and 'super-patriotic nonsense'.[9]

Buttrick's approach was a significant attempt to adapt classical rhetoric for contemporary situations by stressing both movement and cohesion and highlighting the importance of a thought-through structure for the sermon as well as the significance and power of language. However, too many moves that are not carefully linked can lead to a disjointed sermon, while a good preacher should on occasions be able to hold a congregation's attention for longer while an idea is discussed.

Thomas Long's book *The Witness of Preaching*[10] develops the idea that to preach is to bear witness, thus emphasizing the authority of the preacher who speaks of what he or she has seen and heard (unlike a messenger who is entrusted with someone else's message to report). The preacher must learn to listen to the Bible and the congregation, and to choose the best words and patterns to convey his or her discoveries. Long's particular contribution to the evolving approach to homiletics is the emphasis on the focus and function in the sermon, both of which grow out of the exegesis of the biblical text. The focus is the concise description of what the sermon is about and the function is expressed in the preacher's hopes for what it will do in and for the hearers. Both should relate to each other and be clear and relatively simple: Long criticizes complex and rigid structures of deductive preaching which produce turgid, static sermons that are essentially a series of propositions presented rationally. Instead he wants the preacher to give intentional thought to the form of this particular sermon, taking account of the shape of the gospel being proclaimed and the way this congregation listens, so that the resulting sermon invites, even demands, that the hearers listen in the way the preacher intends. This means facing questions that rarely arose for deductive preachers: how to begin the sermon and which form would best enable the hearers to be active and creative listeners.[11] Long has the arresting thought that when pilgrims embark on a journey they hold in common only a destination; when they reach the end of the journey they share a common life and the preacher's task is to facilitate the emergence of that common life, through the sermon.[12] This is much more exciting than preparing a three-point deductive sermon for people to take or leave individually.

Eugene Lowry follows Craddock in adopting a problem-solving approach to preaching but shifts the problem from Craddock's question of the text's contemporary meaning to that of the 'felt need' of the hearers. Arguing that 'a good sermon is one that will command the active attention of every listener', Lowry thinks it is best to begin with any problem or dilemma the hearers face, since that guarantees attention. In this 'itch and scratch' approach, the preacher pushes a problem against the gospel to see if the interaction produces a sermon. To do this, the preacher must be aware where the congregation or the world is itching and scratch that point with the Scriptures, 'Sermons are born when at least implicitly in the preacher's mind the problematic *itch* intersects a solutional *scratch* – between the particularity of the human predicament and the particularity of the gospel. It is this intersection (often *felt* rather than known) which produces the sensed certainty that a sermon is about to take shape.'[13]

Roundly rejecting the advice he was given in homiletics classes, 'Tell them what you are going to tell them, tell them, and then tell them what you have told them', Lowry's approach revolves around five movements or stages in the sermon. These are: describing the problem and upsetting the equilibrium;

35

analysing the discrepancy; disclosing the key to resolution; experiencing the gospel; and anticipating the consequences. In essence the sermon begins with the problem, brings the gospel to bear on it so that a surprise resolution is glimpsed, fleshes this out and enables the hearers to apply it to themselves, before finally projecting the gospel's impact into the future so that transformation becomes possible. Lowry recognizes that the first stage may not be necessary – for example, at funerals the coffin is the very tangible reminder that the equilibrium is already upset. The analysis of the discrepancy need not focus on the 'why?' question, but could be 'how?', 'when?' or 'where?' and, particularly in a prophetic sermon, some ambiguity may be needed to avoid defensiveness in the hearers. For Lowry, timing is everything: the denouement of the good news must not be announced too soon because part of the power of the sermon lies in the congregation's experience of the futility of the search before the resolution is reached, although the preacher must give them a sense of direction to keep their interest.[14]

When Lowry learned to preach he was told that Jesus' parables have a single point and the preacher's job was to identify it and develop a sermon around it, without turning the parables into allegories with multiple referents ('this means that'), which only served to confuse. Now he argues that biblical studies tell us that, in Jesus' hands, parables don't *have* a point, they *are* a point which has implications for preaching parables. It is poor theology to say that meaning always stands outside experience: if we cannot catch the meaning of 'neighbour' from inside Jesus' story of the Good Samaritan, we are unlikely to discover it elsewhere. Recognizing that biblical stories come in all shapes and sizes, forms and configurations – some being comic, others tragic; some like riddles, others including clear admonitions – he maintains that they cannot all be handled in the same way but need different sermonic forms.[15] Choosing the form of the sermon is the preacher's central task, and he or she has to be familiar with the text, listening to its blend of knowledge and mystery, grasping and being grasped, managing and being led; in other words, being vulnerable before the biblical story and open to inadvertent surprise. Lowry advocates reading the text out loud in different translations, letting it accost and confront us, looking for trouble – things that don't fit or are weird – exploring it not for its answers but to pursue its problem with the purpose of finding its focus because the identification of conflict or ambiguity needing resolution could lead to the beginning of a sermon. Just as plots in parables have a fundamental turn and never end up as expected – the prodigal decides to return home; Jesus turns the lawyer's question on its head – so do sermons preached on them, and once the focus is clear the next step is to ask, 'What will be its fundamental turn?' That will emerge with further exploration, and where it occurs may determine the narrative sermon form to be used. The final step is to determine the sermon's aim or purpose (Long's function) by asking what we hope will happen as a result of the sermon being preached. Lowry dislikes choosing a *theme* for the sermon, arguing that most preachers promptly lapse into deductive mode, whereas having an *aim* keeps attention on the question rather than the answer.[16]

Lowry identifies three particular pitfalls: omitting the good news, not connecting the good news to our situation and (recognizing that people's attention wavers) not repeating the crucial good news.[17] He offered four approaches to sermon design: running the story, delaying the story, suspending the story and alternating the story. A preacher who is running the story follows it from the text while adding relevant comments. When delaying the story the preacher begins elsewhere, perhaps with a pastoral concern, and allows that context to open up the text in a new way. Suspending the story begins with the text but lets something else happen along the way, for example if the biblical story runs into trouble (Jesus says something inexplicable) which requires investigation the preacher may move away from the text to a contemporary situation or another biblical text in order to shed light on it, before returning to the story. Finally, when alternating the story the preacher divides the story into sections or episodes and fills other material around the biblical story, alternating between the two, although he notes the danger that preachers will generalize its moral each time.[18]

Several other preachers have homed in on ways to recover narrative in preaching. To take one example, Richard Jensen proposes that much of the Bible reflects the story-stitching approach of an oral culture: Jesus told stories to describe the kingdom of God, and the gospel writers stitched together stories about Jesus producing a gospel with episodes rather than a linear plot line, and storytellers want listeners to participate in the world of the story. 'A return to the world of story in our preaching is so vital today. The gospel message told in story form invites people to participate in the very reality of its life.' He suggests making the whole sermon into a story and, citing the example of Garrison Keillor's stories on the radio, suggests that we listen intently because we enjoy the story itself, not because we want to move towards resolutions, and we go to Lake Wobegon in our imaginations and know the people. *The Archers* does the same in Britain. Very particular stories of very particular people strike a universal chord, and Jensen concludes that in preaching the particular is the best way to the universal. He emphasizes the role of repetition in storytelling and its continued use in the African-American preaching tradition.[19] He urges preachers to work on their narrative skills before trying them out in the pulpit since we know a good storyteller when we hear one: in my local library a storyteller was delayed and a staff member tried to keep the children's attention with a story, but to little effect and the library rang with the sounds of bored children. As soon as the storyteller arrived the atmosphere was transformed and silence descended. His opening lines told me that here was someone who knew what he was doing. Storytelling takes practice.

Arguing that we are in a post-literate culture, Jensen refuses to be daunted by the challenges of electronic forms of communication and pleads for a return to the tradition of thinking in story. He describes a series he preached on the Lord's Prayer with biblical stories to throw light on each petition (for example, the parable of the prodigal son for the petition 'forgive us our sins as we forgive those who sin against us'), in which he put the sermon together by thinking in biblical story. His hearers appreciated it and Jensen suggests that we should fill people's heads not just with ideas but with people, bringing the characters of the Bible alive for them.[20]

It could be argued that changes in preaching styles since the 1960s represent a shift from left-brained thinking to right-brained thinking, with the resulting question of whether something valuable has been lost in the process: surely there are times and places where the deductive, left-brained approach is most appropriate? Jensen's answer is not to dismiss preaching based on the world of print since, for didactic biblical texts, storytelling is not an appropriate sermonic form and some audiences are still at home in a literate environment with its logical presentation of ideas. So sometimes the faithful response is to teach rather than tell stories – he cites a series of sermons on grief.[21] Adequate grounding in rhetoric, as it plays out in various forms of preaching, allows informed decisions about the appropriate style of preaching.

What would Psalm 137 with its question about singing the Lord's song in a strange land look like if preached using these approaches? The first question would be the focus and function of the sermon – perhaps how to keep faith in a time of trouble. After that the form of the sermon would be considered: Buttrick would have a series of snapshots of the exiles – first back in Jerusalem before the fall of the city, then mocked by the Babylonians, then refusing to sing before finally turning to God in distress – and end by making links to how we can face crisis with God; Long would probably engage the hearers in a conversation with the exiles with the aim of leading them to strengthened faith in God in the midst of distress, whereas Lowry would begin with a problem and apply the insights of the psalm to that, leading to the hope of transformation for people trapped in the crisis. Jensen would advise telling the story of the exiles as story, perhaps alternating it with a contemporary situation. The possibilities are considerable and the whole thing is vastly more dynamic than a propositional discourse.

Notes

1 Richard Jensen, *Thinking in Story: Preaching in a Post-Literate Age*, CSS, Lima, OH, 1995, pp. 28–30, 34–8.

2 Sangster himself identified the difference between deductive and inductive preaching, but it is Craddock who gave inductive preaching its language and momentum. An even earlier forerunner of the inductive method of preaching can be seen in some of the insights of François Fénelon in the eighteenth century, and even in Aristotle's *Rhetoric*, where he argues that rhetorical argument begins with the common beliefs (the *endoxa*) of the hearers.

3 Fred Craddock, *As One Without Authority*, Abingdon Press, Nashville, 1971, pp. 124–5.

4 Paul Marshall comments, 'The hallmark of biblical preaching is the fact that what is preached is determined by the content of the text . . . Preaching is biblical when the sermon has the same function as the text.' Paul Marshall, *Preaching for the Church Today*, Church Hymnal Corporation, New York, 1990, p. 73.

5 Fred Craddock, *Preaching*, Abingdon Press, Nashville, 1985, pp. 17–18.

6 Craddock, *Preaching*, pp. 21–7.

7 see, for example, Susan Durber, *Preaching Like a Woman*, SPCK, London, 2007.

8 David Buttrick, *Homiletic: Moves and Structures*, Fortress Press, Philadelphia, 1987.

9 Buttrick, *Homiletic*, pp. 37–53.

10 Thomas Long, *The Witness of Preaching*, Westminster John Knox, Louisville, 1989, pp. 46–7.

11 Long, *Witness of Preaching*, pp. 104–11.

12 Long, *Witness of Preaching*, p. 189.

13 Eugene Lowry, *The Homiletical Plot: The Sermon as Narrative Art Form*, John Knox, Atlanta, 1980, 2001, pp. 2, 18–19. Emphases in the original.

14 Lowry, *Homiletical Plot*, pp. 21, 92, 94, 76, 38.

15 Eugene Lowry, *How to Preach a Parable: Design for Narrative Sermons*, Abingdon Press, Nashville, 1989, pp. 19–20, 23, 27.

16 Lowry, *How to Preach a Parable*, pp. 32–36.

17 Lowry, *How to Preach a Parable*, pp. 22, 25.

18 Lowry, *How to Preach a Parable*, pp. 38–41. Lowry provides sermons which illustrate each approach.

19 Richard Jensen, *Thinking in Story*, pp. 23–5.

20 Jensen, *Thinking in Story*, pp. 95–96.

21 Jensen, *Thinking in Story*, pp. 29, 39, 57.

4

THE CALLING TO PREACH

'My heart is astir with gracious words; as I make my song for the king, my tongue is the pen of a ready writer' (Psalm 45.1; *Common Worship*). That is what it means to be a preacher – to have a heart astir, a song of gracious words and speech ready to flow. We need all three.

I once asked an artist how long it took to do a particular piece of work and the answer was 'a lifetime'. It is the same with preaching: every sermon is the product of a lifetime. John Killinger has written,

There are few vocations in which the character and inner life of the persons are as important as they are in the ministry. To preach well Sunday after Sunday preachers must be in touch with the deepest resources of their beings. Their spirits must be whole and alert, sensitive to inner feelings and to the needs of others. They must be relaxed enough to draw upon all their wit and knowledge, yet excited enough to leap beyond the given sum total of their powers and produce sermons that are obviously 'given by God'. There is no profession in which performance depends so much upon the accumulation of insight and information. Good preaching is a matter of overflow – of having one's mood and spirit so primed with reading and experience that they simply rise up in weekly rhythm to produce a Nilotic blessing of the environment.[1]

Who we are influences how we preach, and what we do in private will be revealed in how we preach in public; the sermon is but the tip of the iceberg. Aristotle believed that a person's moral character was the most effective evidence in making his or her proof, and rhetorical theory claims that our knowledge of human character is the ground of persuasion because it enables us to shape our arguments appropriately. Augustine argued that the preacher's life, or ethos, determined whether he would be heard and affected the message.[2] Preaching adds a public dimension to our character: people read us as well as hear our sermons.

Preaching involves encounter between people. Phillips Brooks's famous definition of preaching, 'the communication of truth by man to men', or 'truth through personality', has stood the test of time even though it is incomplete, the language is dated and it leaves much undefined.[3] Brooks added,

> The truth must come through the person, not merely over his lips, not merely into his understanding and out through his pen. It must come through his character, his affections, his whole intellectual and moral being. It must come genuinely through him . . . Preparation for ministry . . . must be nothing less than the kneading and tempering of a man's whole nature till it becomes of such consistence and quality as to be capable of transmission. This is the largeness of the preacher's culture.[4]

He spoke of the preacher's life as one of large accumulation, always seeking and owning the truth out of which sermons will make themselves.[5] When ordaining people, the bishop seeks public assurance that they will go on being 'diligent in prayer, in reading Holy Scripture, and in all studies that will deepen your faith and fit you to bear witness to the truth of the gospel' as well as fashioning their lives according to the way of Christ so that they may be a pattern and example to Christ's people.[6] Brooks described the difference between a sermon by a preacher whom the gospel has come over, which 'reaches us tinged and flavoured with his superficial characteristics, belittled with his littleness', and one by a preacher whom the gospel comes through, 'and we receive it impressed and winged with all the earnestness and strength there is in him'.[7]

Preaching responsibilities are not listed as a neat and tidy section of a job description but are integral to a way of life that is given to the service of God and other people,[8] so, when ordaining people in the Church of England, the bishop asks if those to be ordained are not only of sound learning but have been found to be of godly life. The ministry of priests includes being shepherds, messengers, watchmen, stewards of the Lord, proclaiming the word of the Lord, teaching, admonishing, feeding and providing for the people. It also includes searching out the lost, calling them to repentance and declaring the forgiveness of sins. Priests tell the story of God's love with all God's people, nurture people in the faith, unfold the Scriptures, preach the word in and out of season, lead people in worship, bless them and minister to them in need.[9] This can be summed up in the concept of the preacher as the parish theologian whose responsibility is both to tend the faithful in their Christian lives and to take the gospel beyond the church doors since preachers are charged by the Church with the public duty to tell the Church's story.[10]

Preaching is part of this much broader ordained ministry, as it is in other churches, while Readers in the Church of England also have wider responsibilities related to leading worship. Hensley Henson, a former Bishop of Durham, wrote, 'Of all the actions of Christian ministry, preaching is the highest, and the test of our reverence for our profession is our performance of the preacher's duty.'[11] According to Thomas Long the preacher never goes to the Scriptures alone because the Church goes to the Scriptures by means of the preacher, so preaching is not merely a deed performed by an individual preacher but the faithful action of the whole Church.[12] Preaching is not a task we take on ourselves as an end in itself but is part of the calling to care for the Church and go in search of the lost (mountain rescue and lifeboats come to mind). It is linked with nurture and guidance as well as teaching and admonition, and it is part of collaborative ministry undertaken with church leaders and all God's people. It flows from a life that has ethical, social and devotional backbone and is open to the guidance of the Holy Spirit. It is not stretching the point to say that preachers are not called so much to preach sermons as to live lives which nurture and bear witness to the words they say in the pulpit. In offering ourselves for this ministry we accept the demands of self-discipline and openness to the empowering of the Holy Spirit, who will renew us in holiness.[13] This is demanding and will not always meet with evident success; Sangster notes how depressing it can be to pour out one's soul week after week to a small group of people who never seem to be affected by what they hear. In those circumstances the preacher must guard periods of daily devotion with jealous care, otherwise work will become simply a dull routine in which 'Nothing ever happens, and – worse still – he no longer thinks it will.'[14] Timothy Radcliffe's summary is apposite: 'Becoming a preacher is more than learning a certain amount of information, so that you may have something to say, and a few preaching techniques so that you know how to say it. It is being formed as someone who can hear the Lord and speak a word that offers life.'[15]

The character of those called to preach

Paul's message was simply 'Christ, and him crucified' (1 Corinthians 2.2) or 'Jesus Christ as Lord and ourselves as your slaves for Jesus' sake' (2 Corinthians 4.5), and he specifically said, 'we do not proclaim ourselves'. But in other letters he exhorted his readers to 'join in imitating me, and observe those who live according to the example you have in us' (Philippians 3.17) and 'as you learned from us how you ought to live and to please God . . . you should do so more and more' (1 Thessalonians 4.1). He also dared to say that he prayed that King Agrippa might become such as he was, except for his chains (Acts 26.29). Paul's message was Jesus Christ, but he knew that his way of life was integral to the vocation to preach the gospel and an illustration of the message. Before we can preach to others, our own lives must be addressed by God's word, and Nicola Slee reminds us of the background work that is necessary if we are to be people who carve out the space to hear the word of God:

> Hearing the word, really hearing it with our whole being, is something both utterly simple and extremely hard. It is both gift and labour: something we have to work at, both collectively and individually; and something we do not deserve or earn but is graciously given to us out of God's abundance. Our part is to do all we can to make space for the word to be spoken, to cultivate the habits and disciplines that will allow the word to be heard: it is up to God, in God's freedom, to speak as and when God wills.[16]

Paul named some qualities the Church can expect to see in lives thus open to God. He distinguished the works of the flesh (plural and related to actions) from the fruit of the Spirit (singular and related to being) which is an integrated and integral element of character. A preacher bearing the fruit of the Spirit lives a life marked by love, joy, peace, patience, kindness, generosity, faithfulness, gentleness and self-control. We can't settle for some and let ourselves off the hook for the rest. Paul reminds us that if we are led by the Spirit then our desires are opposed to the works of the flesh: fornication, impurity, licentiousness, idolatry, sorcery, enmities, strife, jealousy, anger, quarrels, dissensions, factions, envy, drunkenness and carousing (Galatians 5.17–23). An honest health check against that list is a salutary Lenten practice for preachers because of that link between our private and public lives.[17] At the very heart of it all is the vocation to holiness of life.

Our preaching grows from our own relationship with God. The psalmist calls us to run in the way of God's commandments (Psalm 119.32) and Augustine, in his treatise on preaching, explained what this meant for one who is called to preach.

Now a man speaks with more or less wisdom just as he has made more or less progress in the knowledge of Scripture; I do not mean by reading them much and committing them to memory, but by understanding them aright and carefully searching into their meaning. For there are who read and yet neglect them; they read to remember the words, but are careless about knowing the meaning. It is plain we must set far above these the men who are not so retentive of the words, but see with the eyes of the heart into the heart of Scripture. Better than either of these, however, is the man who, when he wishes, can repeat the words, and at the same time correctly apprehends their meaning.[18]

Calvin Miller's words are challenging: 'A good preacher brings to the pulpit good sermons from his private devotion. A great preacher brings to the pulpit great sermons from the presence of God.'[19] Unwittingly what we say will bear the hallmarks of our fidelity to the Christian tradition and the freshness of our vibrant exposure to the God who is beyond our knowing. No wonder the bishop asks those to be ordained if they will be diligent in prayer, in reading Holy Scripture, and in all studies that will deepen their faith and fit them to bear witness to the truth of the gospel. Preachers must be knowledgeable students of God's word: ongoing disciplined and informed study is called for, but note that it is all studies, not just biblical or theological studies – the field is wide and we can all find areas for study to enthral and stimulate us. Sadly, too often the situation has changed little since R. W. Dale's 1878 lament about preachers whose sermons are like the conversations of people who have never left their village or county and want to settle the affairs of nations as if they were parochial business.[20] In her wise novel *Gilead*, Marilynne Robinson puts these words onto the lips of an elderly preacher, speaking of his preacher father who eventually left the small town where he had lived all his life:

He was expounding the wonders of the larger world, and I was resolving in my heart never to risk the experience of them. He said 'I have become aware that we lived here within the limits of notions that were very old and even very local. I want you to understand that you do not have to be loyal to them.'[21]

As he hinted, the son could not rise to the challenge and, inevitably, at the end of the novel the wider world comes to him in a poignantly demanding way.

At times we will need the courage to tell the difficult truth with compassion and empathy for our hearers as well as firmness without authoritarianism. Firmness includes firmness with ourselves and with the boundaries that we set for our belief (for example the authority of Scripture and of creedal beliefs) which allows those listening to trust us when we lead them on the sermon's journey of exploration. Since it goes without saying that we have a duty not to preach heresy (although I have heard occasional sermons come perilously, but probably innocently, close to that), serious study of the Bible and of theology are a *sine qua non* of preaching. We are not self-appointed or freelance preachers but inhabit a denominational tradition and, in giving us authority to preach, the Church exercises authority over us.[22] In accepting the calling to preach we accept with it the responsibility to grow in the tradition of which we are part. We do this on behalf of the people we serve who are at our elbow when we study the Bible, reminding us of their life situations which they hope our preaching will touch; when we read a theological book, they are asking us questions that the book may help us to answer; when we pray, they are there with their needs. When we study on behalf of the people who will hear us it is just as much a priestly act as administering the sacraments or offering pastoral care.

Faith, love of life, graciousness, respect for other people, courage, sincerity, lightness of touch, honesty, delight, passion, an enquiring mind that is open to surprise, wonder and awe: the list of attributes could go on. At stake in all of this is our Christian integrity. We are works in progress, pilgrims alongside those who hear us preach. Before there can be a sermon that lives and breathes and has effect there has to be a preacher who has prayed for God to

> Kindle a flame of sacred love
> on the mean altar of my heart.
> There let it for thy glory burn
> with inextinguishable blaze.[23]

We won't have to tell people the state of our spiritual lives, they will know. We will face doubts and intellectual questions in our Christian life, but the study not the pulpit is the place to face them head on. Calvin Miller observes astutely,

> Sermons take their life from the nearness of God . . . When preachers lose track of God, their sermons get pushier. Not only that, when God is most absent in their lives they are all the more present. The quieter God gets, the louder they get . . . so we lose God when he's quiet, because we're too loud. We run from him when he gets loud, because we cannot stand the storm of his coming. Either way, we often come to the pulpit without him, having no clear remembrance of our last real conversation.[24]

Like it or not, some people will put us on pedestals. If we try to deny it or let it go to our heads we are in danger, but if we can accept that given authority peacefully and prayerfully, taking responsibility for knowing ourselves and being committed to God, then our ethos will be such that the congregation can flourish. As Michael Sadgrove has written,

> Wisdom, in the Hebrew Bible, means knowing oneself as a public figure in a role, and as a human person; therefore knowing oneself means understanding and living out with integrity the often difficult relationship between the two. Here, the pastoral care of the clergy, linked to wise support and mentoring, are indispensable not only for their own mental and spiritual health but for the wellbeing of the whole church.[25]

Emotional maturity frees us to experience and express emotions appropriately – from intense joy to profound grief. We are human and there are times when we are rightly emotional, for example if we have been bereaved. We are responsible for tending our emotional needs when we are out of the pulpit or they will express themselves, inappropriately and unexpectedly, in the pulpit, possibly by uncontrollable emotions that embarrass and anger people or force them in to pastoral care mode on our behalf, or by dogmatism born of attempts at repression. If we find ourselves being so dogmatic about something that we can broach no other viewpoint it is time to check whether this is valid certainty or an attempt to silence something we cannot face in ourselves.[26] We have different personalities from each other and self-awareness involves knowing ourselves and taking ourselves seriously yet lightly, not forever measuring ourselves enviously against others.[27] This includes knowing our reasonable need for sleep, good diet, exercise, recreation and fun, cultural nourishment, prayer, sociability and solitude. We can and should seek out beauty in our lives, things that make us laugh, sing or dance, as well as beautiful and creative words in literature and poetry. If we are perpetually dour in the pulpit, why, given that we are charged with the proclamation of good news of great joy? Self-aware people also know when it is or is not appropriate to be self-disclosing in a sermon or when our experience is not adequate to be drawn on.

Self-disclosure

Being accessible to others requires that we set boundaries in our lives to protect ourselves.[28] A question of accessibility that relates specifically to preaching is, 'If who we are is an essential element of our preaching, should we talk about ourselves from the pulpit?' There are many perspectives on this. A starting-point for consideration is that we cannot preach at all unless we reveal ourselves to some extent – even Paul did it.[29] The reason for this it is that we are neither acting nor lecturing but preaching. Phillips Brooks reminds us,

> Preaching is the communication of truth by man to men. It has in it two essential elements, truth and personality. Neither of these can it spare and still be preaching. The truest truth, the most authoritative statement of God's will, communicated in any other way than through the personality of brother man to men is not preached truth . . . And preaching is the bringing of truth through personality.[30]

We cannot preach unless we are prepared for God to be forever prising our life open. So, whether life is uncontainable joy, an aching struggle or a pedestrian trudge, when we stand in the pulpit we bring not just our words but our life and we lay ourselves open to God and the congregation even if we say nothing confessional. Congregations can and will read us and our body language. They will see beyond our nerves or our confidence and pick up our approach to God's word, our faith, our concern for their well-being and our grasp of what is going on in their lives. They will know if we have dared to face their real issues and questions, bringing them to our prayerful engagement with Scripture on their behalf, or have resorted to other people's generalities. They will also know if we dream of spiritual greatness for them, enlarging their vision and deepening their faith, or if we have no particular sense of where we are leading them. They will also listen for what we never say from the pulpit. All this will come across loud and clear whether or not we utter one word about ourselves.

Therefore the question of whether or not to self-disclose in preaching is better reframed as a question about the extent and manner of our self-disclosure. Exhibitionism is ruled out because people come to church to hear and draw closer to God, not to us. Nevertheless, as Brooks insists, the preached truth must come through us as people, and that may involve occasionally talking about God's work in our own lives. After all, theologically we proclaim God incarnate among us, God who took human flesh and dwelt among us, God who continues to live and work in and through humans today. We have a story to tell of God's grace revealed in us since we are participants in God's work in our world. That is not, however, licence to drip-feed enough material over the weeks for people to construct our life history. A rule of thumb is to be ruthless about not mentioning ourselves unless we are sure that doing so will help the message of the sermon and not shift the focus of the sermon from God to us.[31]

The pulpit should not be the only place where we talk about ourselves, but there are times when it can help to use our own experience in order to put flesh on the bones of what we are trying to say, so long as any story about ourselves is about God's work in our lives and is told carefully so that we are portrayed neither as a hero of the faith nor as a weak failure – in both cases the congregation is left unsure how to relate to us. Personal struggles should not be discussed unless and until we can talk about them appropriately and can convey clearly that they are no longer a dominating influence in our lives. This frees the congregation not to respond to the particular situation but to hear it as an example of God's work through past events. If we need pastoral care or counselling ourselves we should find it in appropriate places and not make a veiled plea for it from the pulpit, thus confusing our relationship with the congregation.

There are times when something undramatic that happened to us in daily life may be a fruitful illustration, and preparation for preaching includes attentiveness to our lives. Thus I started a sermon about walking by faith,

If you visit a certain National Trust property not too far from here, which is known for its extensive grounds that are ideal for long walks, you may discover, as I did, that whoever did the signage expects everyone to walk in an anticlockwise direction. Not intending to be perverse, I walked clockwise, and although I saw several signs with arrows on over the course of about six miles, none of them told me which way to go. Instead they all pointed back the way I had come, thus confirming to me that I had come from the right direction but leaving me to make my own decisions about where to go next at junctions. It was a fascinating exercise to discover that there was not a single sign for clockwise walkers!

I found myself recalling that experience when I looked at today's reading from Hebrews. 'Faith is the assurance of things hoped for, the conviction of things not seen. By faith Abraham obeyed when he was called to set out not knowing where he was going.' He only found out as he went along that he was going the right way. Otherwise there would have been no faith involved, just the spiritual equivalent of the willingness to follow directional arrows. That's easier, but it's not an act of faith.[32]

Some practical considerations: always obtain people's permission before telling stories that involve them and tell the congregation that you have it; never betray confidences from the pulpit because in an instant trust is betrayed not only with the person whose story is being told but also with the congregation who will fear the disclosure of their secrets from the pulpit – all we have revealed about ourselves is our pastoral untrustworthiness. If it is impossible to obtain permission but the story is vital to the sermon, disguise all details of names, place, time and anything else that will hint at identity, and say that you are doing so to prevent people trying to identify the person.

Overuse of our stories makes us the filter for all we say about God, disempowers hearers whose experience does not match ours, and may make us indispensable to others. However, if we never refer to ourselves in our sermons, the congregation is entitled to wonder if we know what we are talking about or if we are relying on abstract words and ideas. The Bible is full of stories of God's word being revealed in and through people's lives; we are just one more in the chain and the question is whether our particular experience is helpful in any particular sermon. Perhaps a more important question concerns the kind of life that we lead – do we have any stories to tell of God's gracious working in our lives?

Preaching and authority

Preachers have to be comfortable with authority: the authority that has authorized them to preach, the authority of Scripture, and the authority that is given to them by their hearers. Discomfort with any of these will cause shipwreck for the preacher or the hearers. Part of learning to preach is learning to inhabit authority appropriately. Behind Trollope's amusing words quoted in the introduction to this book lies the truth that people do give preachers authority, the source of which varies. While all Christian preaching is predicated on the authority of Scripture (although there may be different interpretations of the same Scripture, its authority is not at stake), different styles of preaching will draw on different forms of given authority. John McClure identifies some of these sources of given authority as the traditional authority of the preaching office, the relationship of preacher and the biblical text, professional competence, giftedness or charisma, the preacher's commitment to God's power and mighty acts in history (in the black preaching tradition), the preacher's star quality (particularly in revivalist traditions), relational authority arising from pastoral and personal relationships and (particularly in prophetic traditions of preaching) the authority of being a living oracle of God.[33]

Mature Christian character is needed if that authority is not to be abused, assumed inappropriately, or denied inappropriately. In the twentieth century the previous emphasis on the character of the preacher was at times called into question – Karl Barth downplayed it in his emphasis on preaching biblically grounded messages – but there is now wide recognition that the character of the preacher is an integral part of homiletics and therefore worthy of our constant attention. People will know if the words we preach have taken root in our lives, been honed through our experience, and are bearing the fruit of the Spirit. The calling to preach is not just about words spoken from a pulpit, it is about a life in which the fire of God is kindled. To preach is to be on both the giving and receiving end of grace.[34]

Notes

1 John Killinger, *Fundamentals of Preaching*, SCM Press, London, 1985, pp. 187–8.

2 Augustine, *On Christian Doctrine*, 4.59.

3 Thus, Donald Coggan raises questions about the adequacy of much of this: What is truth? What kind of man? Can anyone preach? If not, what are the essential qualifications which go to the making of a preacher without which he can only *talk*? Donald Coggan, *Stewards of Grace*, Hodder & Stoughton, London, 1958, p. 24.

4 Phillips Brooks, *Lectures on Preaching (1877)*, H. R. Allenson, London, 1895, pp. 8, 9.

5 Brooks, *Lectures on Preaching*, p. 159.

6 Summarized from *Common Worship, The Order of Priests, also called Presbyters*. Copyright © The Archbishops' Council 2005.

7 Brooks, *Lectures on Preaching*, pp. 5, 8, 9.

8 Michael Monshau notes that in Hebrew antiquity, a person's words were not typically understood to be separate from the speaker's own person. One's words were perceived to convey the expression of one's own self. Michael Monshau (ed.), *Preaching at the Double Feast: Homiletics for Eucharistic Worship*, Liturgical Press, Collegeville, MN, 2006, p. 2.

9 See *Common Worship, The Order of Priests, also called Presbyters*, for the full description of the ministry of priests.

10 I am indebted to Michael Sadgrove for this summary of the ordinal's much longer charge to priests.

11 Hensley Henson, *The Church and Parson in England*, Hodder & Stoughton, London, 1927, p. 153.

12 Thomas Long, *The Witness of Preaching*, Westminster John Knox, Louisville, 1989, pp. 46–7.

13 This is spelled out in the questions the bishop puts to those who are to be ordained, about their willingness to order every aspect of their lives in appropriate ways.

14 W. E. Sangster, *The Craft of the Sermon*, Epworth Press, London, 1954, p. 13.

15 Timothy Radcliffe, *Sing a New Song: the Christian Vocation*, Dominican Publications, Dublin, 1999, p. 179.

16 Nicola Slee, 'Word', in Stephen Burns (ed.), *Journey*, Canterbury Press, Norwich, 2008, p. 40.

17 For examples of the characteristics a preacher should embody see, for example, Long, *Witness of Preaching*, p. 21; and James Lapsley 'Personality' in William Willimon and Richard Lischer (eds), *Concise Encyclopaedia of Preaching*, Westminster John Knox Press, Louisville, 1995, pp. 373–4.

18 Augustine, *On Christian Doctrine* 4.5.7.

19 Calvin Miller, *The Sermon Maker: Tales of a Transformed Preacher*, Zondervan, Grand Rapids, 2002, p. 121.

20 R. W. Dale, *Nine Lectures on Preaching*, Barnes, New York, 1878, pp. 109–10. Quoted in Killinger, *Fundamentals of Preaching*, p. 196. These were the 1878 Lyman Beecher lectures at Yale Divinity School.

21 Marilynne Robinson, *Gilead*, Virago, London, 2005, p. 269.

22 Hence the bishop's question to those to be ordained, 'Will you accept and minister the discipline of this Church, and respect authority duly exercised within it?'

23 Charles Wesley. 'O Thou, who camest from above'.

24 Miller, *Sermon Maker*, pp. 16, 18.

25 Michael Sadgrove, *Wisdom and Ministry*, SPCK, London, 2008, p. 10.

26 In *Hamlet*, Gertrude in her (usually misquoted) line, 'The lady doth protest too much, methinks' said that the Player Queen's vows were so intense and so repeated that their credibility was called into question ('protest' originally meant 'declare solemnly').

27 Resources like the Enneagram and Myers Briggs personality tests have wide literatures, including, in relation to preaching, Leslie Francis and Andrew Village, *Preaching with all our Souls*, Continuum, London, 2008. David Schlafer, *Your Way with God's Word*, Cowley, Cambridge, MA, 1995, is a helpful guide to discovering our own distinctive preaching voice.

28 See Christopher Cocksworth and Rosalind Brown, *Being a Priest Today*, Canterbury Press, London, 2003, 2007, pp. 138–9.

29 Craddock argues that all preaching is to some extent self-disclosure by the preacher, and that this is simply a truth about communication. Fred Craddock, *Preaching*, Abingdon Press, Nashville, 1985, p. 23.

30 Brooks, *Lectures on Preaching (1877)*, pp. 5, 8.

31 For an appropriate example, given both the context of the sermon and his own history, see Michael Mayne, 'The Festival of the Sons of the Clergy', 14 May 1996, in Horace Dammers (ed.), *Preaching from the Cathedrals*, Mowbray, London, 1998, pp. 59–63.

32 Durham Cathedral Sermons: 12 August 2007. The same sermon contains a further example of self-disclosure, this time referring to deci-

sions I made in the past that influenced the direction of my life. I chose to do this because it gave a concrete example of what I was speaking about.

33 John S. McClure, *Preaching Words: 144 Key Terms in Homiletics*, Westminster John Knox, Louisville, 2007, pp. 7–9.

34 Michael Sadgrove, *On Preaching*, unpublished address to Wakefield Diocesan Clergy.

5

IMAGINATION TRANSFORMED

The Wonder of the Preacher

Another aspect of our character as preachers is imagination: it is God's gift and vital in preaching. So often we are bound by the predictable. Ronald Blythe describes what happens when imagination is yielded to God; he is describing a hymn, but the same is true of a sermon,

> Samuel Crossman . . . had written a book called *The Young Man's Meditation*, a collection of poems which included 'My song is love unknown'. He had been reading George Herbert's 'Love unknown' and Herbert had been reading Psalm 51. For that is what happens to divine love. It streams through the imagination of poets, rhyming up here and there, catching a tune, catching a congregation.[1]

Another way of putting it is to say that we are privileged in preaching to compose a new harmony or descant to God's eternal melody of love, as we attempt to express the intangible through the tangible. A member of the Durham Cathedral community once described the experience of being in the Cathedral crossing under the tower as 'Your fingertips are resting on glory, it's like living on the edge of eternity'[2] and it can be the same with language: there are moments when we are hovering on the edge of glory as God takes our words and uses them as icons of his grace. We cannot manufacture these times but we can be open to this transfiguration of human language when godly imagination has found a new way to articulate wonder.

God's creation of the world was the ultimate act of imagination – God spoke and worlds came to be. Jesus coaxed the disciples into using their imagination: he showed them flowers, and they found themselves thinking about King Solomon and the extent of their own trust in God (Matthew 6.28–29). Amos was shown a plumbline (Amos 7.8) and suddenly discovered a world of judgement and desolation, and when he saw a basket of summer fruit (Amos 8.2), the Lord used a pun (lost to us in translation but indicated in the footnotes) to say the end was coming on the people of Israel. Jesus asked many questions, sometimes answering questions with questions, forcing people to think expansively and creatively. The Holy Spirit is unpredictable: creating disturbances as wind and fire, soothing as a dove, or coming in a still small voice, which we have to be silent to hear. Preaching thrives on creative imagination that helps us to express theoretical ideas concretely and give entirely new perspectives on the over-familiar. Emily Dickinson grasped the idea when she wrote,

> Tell all the Truth, but tell it slant –
> Success in Circuit lies
> Too bright for our infirm Delight
> The Truth's superb surprise
> As Lightning to the Children eased
> With explanation kind
> The Truth must dazzle gradually
> Or every man be blind –

The world is crammed full of wonder, holy places and holy people, as well as dreadful events and human wickedness. All these can and should make our eyes blink and our ears tingle as God's grace crashes against human life. We can't take the risk of ceasing to be astonished by God but, like the poet Anna Kamieńska, are called to be faithful to our first astonishments[3] as we recognize the signs that God might be making the equivalent of a bishop or knight's move in chess, rather than the conventional move of a pawn.

Cultivating our imagination is rather like practising the scales on the piano, except it is much more exciting. It is also, at times, gloriously humorous, and we should not fear appropriate humour in preaching; used carefully it can get under people's defences and unlock their hearts. Michel Quoist's classic *Prayers of Life* includes his prayerful, imaginative wondering about things like green blackboards, wire fences, telephones, bald heads and the sea. His approach was, 'If we knew how to look at life through God's eyes, all of life would become a sign. If we knew how to listen, all of life would become a prayer.'[4] A simple way to start is to spend five minutes simply observing something – a flower, a stone, even a brick wall – just noting what is there: the beauty or drabness of its colours, its delicacy or robustness, its fragrance or the stench, so that, if you were to close your eyes, you would be able to see it in your mind's eye. Taste it, feel it, smell it. Then spend five minutes letting your mind wander around what you have observed, going where your thoughts lead: what ideas does the vein in the stone evoke? What tragedies and triumphs has that old stone wall lived through? Am I the first person ever to have seen the stamen of that flower? Finally spend five minutes letting your imagination and observation suggest things about God, about us, about the world, about life. Are there connections to Scripture to explore? If two people do this, shared thoughts can be developed. We may be surprised what emerges in those 15 minutes. Try it when next preaching from a text about rocks, foundations, the sea or anything that has a physical expression.

We proclaim a gospel of transformation and new life, the kingdom of God coming on earth as in heaven. What does that look like? Walter Brueggemann sees preaching as 'an event in transformed imagination' where preachers do not describe a gospel-governed world but help the congregation to imagine it.[5] He challenges us to use new language, to listen to Scripture and to the world, to set up conversations between them, and dares us to expand our language to incorporate poetic language so that our prose takes wings. When the preacher comes as poet, 'the world is set loose towards healing'.[6] Elsewhere he writes, 'I am increasingly convinced . . . that people are changed not by ethical urging but by transformed imagination.'[7] Nevertheless, we cannot let our imaginations run riot and they have to be in symbiotic relationship with the Christian tradition,[8] if we are to grasp the thrill of God at work in human history.

Every preacher needs what used to be called a commonplace book – a place for recording ideas so that they are available when we need them. Computers make this much easier, but some people prefer card indexes or notebooks. I keep a computer file of quotations; make pencil notes in the margins of books and jot page numbers I might want to return to in pencil on the inside cover along with one or two words to indicate the theme; sometimes type up notes from a book that has been particularly helpful; put pictures and cuttings in an 'ideas' file; and write out by hand using a fountain pen in a good notebook phrases, poems or pictures that I want to return to for my own spiritual nurture whether or not a sermon is in the offing. Whatever its form, keep a commonplace book.

Imagination and words

Words are at the heart of our work. Donald Coggan calls them the chief medium of our message, on a par with wood for the carpenter, clay for the potter and the piano or violin for the musician. He describes them as, 'Sacred things, they need handling with consummate care and with supreme reverence. They are, under the guidance of the Holy Spirit, bearers of the Word.'[9] I would add that we should use words with enjoyment. Good preachers enjoy conversation with other people, listening to others in a way so that when we speak we move the conversation forward. Ideally preaching should pick up the community's conversation before it came to church, add to it and enable it to continue afterward with renewed vigour and insight. Good preaching has a poetic streak. Poetry can help us to speak of what is ineffable, beyond the reach of prose, beyond analysis and in the realm of the heart rather than the mind, but as preachers our prose can also be captivating and life-giving. Our raw materials are words, we can luxuriate in them and fall in love with the dictionary. The former Poet Laureate Andrew Motion describes his wonderful dilemma on dipping into the 13-volume *Oxford English Dictionary*, 'Every time I peer into it, which is several times a day, I think, "All the words I'll ever need are here; the only thing I have to do is get them out in the right order."'[10] Choosing the right word for the meaning we want to convey can be taxing; for T. S. Eliot in 'East Coker', it is an 'intolerable wrestling' but, more hopefully, Seamus Heaney describes a poem by Dylan Thomas as giving 'the sensation of language on the move towards a destination in knowledge'.[11] As preachers it is our joy and privilege to clothe God's word in human speech of the twenty-first century, to allow it to pulsate in our world. Choosing the right words in a world of terse emails presupposes our immersion in fine words, appropriate words, evocative words, that not only say what we need them to say but say it beautifully and winsomely. So taking time to read good words is important for the health of our imaginations, remembering that short stories may be more helpful than essays or long novels as models of language and structure for preachers.[12]

Preachers have to understand the impact of words. Kathleen Norris, in her critique as a poet of the Psalter produced by the International Commission for English in the Liturgy (ICEL), quotes W. H. Auden's definition of poetry as 'memorable speech' and illustrates the power of the memorable or misplaced word in ICEL's texts, pointing out the flaws in some phrases that are suitable for reading but not for speaking. She lends us her poet's ear and both inspires and cautions us in our use of language.[13] Timothy Radcliffe points us to the answer to his question, 'How can any of us get across even the tiniest hint of grace's effervescence?' in his comment that only poets have a chance of communicating 'the dearest freshness deep down things'.[14] The Poetry Translation Centre's fascinating website gives insight into the choice of words as it explains the three stages in the process of translating a poem from one language into another.

> First we look at the original poem: even if most of us can't understand a word, it's always important to hear its music, and to look at how the poet has placed it on the page. Secondly, the language expert produces a literal translation that's as close to the original as possible. And finally, there's the long and detailed negotiation that ends with the translated poem. [This last stage involves] deploying all the resources of English to find words and phrases that are true to the original yet which also convey its special qualities as a poem.[15]

The website provides examples of poems in the stages of translation and illustrates the power of well-chosen words over those that are adequate but flat. Like poets, preachers are always in search of words that are appropriately, but not distractingly, vivid and not only say what is needed but say it imaginatively. Words that are, quite simply, 'right'.

Imaginative words about our world

Lowry begins his sermons with what he describes as the felt need of the hearers. Personally, I prefer to keep that need in dialogue with the Scriptures for the day rather than begin from it, but he presents us with the challenge: do we know the felt need of our hearers? Have we 'felt' the need of our world? Macrina Wiederkehr comments, perhaps on behalf of most of us,

> I have never been very good at feasting on the daily newspaper. It turns in my mouth. This face of suffering I must embrace as my responsibility. Part of the feast is becoming

more aware of the world that is mine. Part of the feast is owning this broken world as my own brokenness. I clasp the newspaper to my heart and ask once again in the stillness of the night. 'What are we doing to the image of God in one another?'[16]

So another way to develop our preaching imagination is to pray imaginatively with the news as we enter the worlds of the people about whom we hear. If words elude you, perhaps music or art will help – what music gives expression to the feelings a news story evokes? What does it look like in art, either your own art or that of someone else? When, living in the USA, I read the *Newsweek* report of the shootings at Columbine High School and looked at the photos of those murdered, I mused onto paper words that explored the devastation of the violent loss of a child. Although I did not refer to it directly, this helped me to walk in the world's shoes that week as I prepared to preach to people whose own experience of the death or criminal acts of their own children might have been evoked by the shootings and brought into church that Sunday. Much later those same musings shed new light on the strong emotions of Psalm 137 when I came to prepare a sermon that did not ignore the anger of its final demanding verses. On another occasion, when the lectionary reading was the story of Lazarus, I put that story in prayerful dialogue with my current experiences as a hospital chaplain, first following the text of John 11 closely and then in freer form as I reflected on the lessons we can learn from cancer. Again, this did not emerge directly in the words of a sermon but it shaped my thinking. John 11 becomes the following on an oncology ward,

> Now certain people, Sarah, Di, Bill, Frank, Rose, Doris, Beth, Chris, Alison, Fred, Kit, Graham, were ill. So they and their families welcomed the chaplain and asked for prayer, 'Lord the one whom we love is ill.' But when the chaplain prayed it seemed God stayed where he was in heaven, and when God got round to answering it was sometimes too late

and some of the people were already in their graves. Their families said to the chaplain, 'If God had been here our loved ones might still have died, but we would not feel so bereft. But even now, we know that God will hear our prayers and give us something of what we ask of him. Help us to pray and face tomorrow.' When the chaplain saw them weeping, she was greatly disturbed in spirit and deeply moved. She began to weep. So some people said, 'See how much she cared.' But others said, 'Could not she, who believed in God, have prayed to God and stopped this person from dying?'[17]

Mercifully, life is not always tragedy and our praying and our preaching can equally be affected if we let our minds wander into glory. So, after watching a sunset in the Rocky Mountains, I wrote:

Pastel haze
erupts into life,
shadows intensify the wonder
as fuchsia and lemon dare to touch.
Sunset.
The heavens declare the glory of God.
Oh! do it again tomorrow![18]

Haiku can be a useful tool for articulating and releasing creativity since they are generally about everyday situations seen in new ways. This Japanese poetic form has been adapted for other languages and comprises three lines of five, seven and five syllables, which, because the word count is so limited, can be a creative way to distil the essence of an experience, highlighting what is most significant. Some of the strict rules governing Japanese haiku have been relaxed, but a haiku normally contains a word that indicates the season in which the haiku is set (thus in the second example below the russet indicates autumn), which can help preachers engage with the liturgical seasons. The following haiku belong in dialogue with Advent and could suggest themes of the suppleness of faithful waiting, or the stripping back to basics that Advent waiting and hoping involves. Both also 'tell it slant' in relation to the exile's experience in Psalm 137.

> The wind roars its power
> jasmine branches rise and fall –
> supple, they withstand.

> A russet carpet –
> woven leaf by flung leaf
> recklessly cascades.[19]

The cinquain, a five-line poem based on a syllable count,[20] is another useful poetic form. Today the strict syllable count tends to be replaced by a word count and the prescription of types of words to be used in order to provide more flexibility. One such pattern is:

> Line 1 – one word, a noun which is either the title or the name of the subject
> Line 2 – three words, adjectives which describe the subject
> Line 3 – two words, multi-syllabic adverbs which describe the verb in line 4
> Line 4 – one word, a verb which describes the subject in line 1
> Line 5 – one word, another noun

As I write this in Advent, the news is full of stories of tragedy from various African countries, in particular the suffering of people caught up in civil wars and forced to flee from their homes either into the bush or into refugee camps.

> Women
> Brutalized, traumatized, fearful,
> Helplessly, desperately
> Flee
> Away

Children
Captured, drugged, enslaved,
Fearfully, unwillingly
Become
Soldiers

The ravaged nation
Gripped by horror cannot hear
Advent's bold challenge

Imaginative words about biblical stories

Good preaching can get under the skin of characters, making
them step out of the page and into our lives. Thomas Troeger
suggests that we should feel the bodily weight of what we are
reading by adopting the bodily posture of the biblical figure we
are describing (or the person in the news), closing our eyes if
the person is blind or lying still if the person is paralysed.[21] A
group of students, some of whom informed me in no uncertain
terms that they couldn't write poetry, had to admit that telling
the passion story in haiku or cinquains helped them enter the
story and released hitherto unsuspected depths in their imagination. Five cinquains from my own passion sequence are:

Mary
hesitant, gracious, daring
boldly, lovingly
anoints
Jesus

Religious leaders
frustrated, angry, impotent
desperately, gleefully
pay
Judas

Cock
scrawny, unseen, alert
noisily, unwittingly
confronts
Peter

Jesus
bleeding, mocked, humiliated
unresistingly, agonizingly
feels
the nails

Mary
startled, confused, abandoned
woefully, tearfully
blurts out
loss

The tight, short structure of haiku and cinquains can be very helpful in focusing our thoughts. Another alternative is to write in a freer form. This example, which addresses Mary at the time of the crucifixion, opens up the raw tension of the situation but, by using the second-person singular, does not attribute feelings to her or put words in her mouth. It was written one year when the Feast of the Annunciation fell in Holy Week and draws on the Collect[22] to reflect on the sharp juxtaposition of the biblical narratives:

O God, by the passion of your blessed Son you made an instrument of shameful death to be for us the means of life: Grant us so to glory in the cross of Christ, that we may gladly suffer shame and loss for the sake of your Son our Saviour Jesus Christ; who lives and reigns with you and the Holy Spirit, one God, for ever and ever. Amen.

Mary, do you remember that
one day a sword would pierce your soul?

And in your darkest nightmare did
you dream that this would be the end?
The son you once held in your arms
is held now by a cross of wood;
the face you once gazed on in love
appears disfigured, crowned with thorns.
The shepherds now are far away
and in their place a shouting mob;
no silent, breathless, timeless awe,
no angel hosts with glorious songs,
no priceless gifts from eastern lands,
but anger, and the stench of death:
the only gift a borrowed tomb,
the only sound a cry of pain.
And is there glory in this cross?
Can you, who sang Magnificat,
rejoiced in God who came to save,
still sing that song, see in this cross
amidst the shame, a Saviour come,
a sign of grace, a means of life?

Mary, once you waited, wept and
bore the pain to bear your son;
now as you stand and wait and weep,
you bear not only pain but shame.
So, is there life amidst this death?
And can you glory in this cross;
mingle your tears with hope
because you know the paradox
that God, your Saviour, first must die?[23]

If words don't come easily, another approach is through
pictures in art. A readily accessible source is the pictures on
Christmas cards. These influence people's thinking about the
nativity story, especially people who have no theological point
of reference and show up once a year at the Midnight service.
Christmas cards rarely locate the nativity in its historical con-

text or grasp its relevance for our contemporary world, so most people visualize Jesus entering either the medieval or Reformation world, or an imaginary world of sugar-sweet Madonnas and child-like shepherds, thus missing entirely the shock that we pray for when singing 'O holy child of Bethlehem . . . be born in us today'. Our visual illiteracy means that the symbolism of the pictures, which earlier ages understood, eludes us: the animals in the stable are not reminders of the prophets' message[24] but appealing additions, while angels convey fictional unreality rather than the transcendence of God breaking into our world. Essentially, the incarnation appears to be neither historical fact nor connected with the reality of the twenty-first century. Maybe it is not insignificant that such images as we do have of Christ born in contemporary surroundings come from the Third World, where liberation theology, with its strong incarnational bias, is an important influence on popular piety. And yet we proclaim, 'Emmanuel, God is with us', knowing that most people envisage something else entirely. Whatever artistic form we use, we are invited – as Jesus invited the disciples – to let our imagination wander and shed light on things in the world and in Scripture, remembering that this will never be the only way we approach Scripture when preparing a sermon: there is always a place for study.

I began one sermon about how we respond when God comes to us, with my reflections arising from time spent prayerfully with my collection of annunciation pictures:

Did Gabriel come half-hurtling in –
wings waving, stirring up the dust
of Galilean tracks you trod (until this day)
with familiar oblivion?
glory trailing in his wake,
did he shine that luminous, incandescent aura
we ascribe to holiness?

Or did he approach with reticent reserve,
gingerly; softening the shock

of the abrupt invasion
of worldly space by heaven's word?
Did he knock, or just unfold
before your startled eyes?

And was he loud, majestic?
messenger of God
more used to fanfares in the heavenly court
than twittering of bird song
in the Galilean hills?
or your first ally in the fear that gripped your heart?
Calling you by name, serene with words of calm
and favour found with God.

Well might you wonder what kind of greeting this might
    be!
Had anything prepared you for this day
when glimpses of God's way of seeing
were unlocked to you,
simple Galilean girl
and favoured one of God?
In Nazareth, whence nothing good can come,
suddenly your home becomes the place where
heaven touches earth,
and neither are the same
again.

Was it request or statement that you heard?
and was there fear or faith within your heart
when you said 'let it be'?
the rising tide of hope and co-creating energy,
welcomed and embraced, 'yes, let it be
with me – with me – according to your word.'
And did you laugh, or cry or pray
when you were left
to wonder at the wonder
of God's grace?[25]

Have you ever wondered just how Gabriel appeared to Mary? Luke leaves the question hanging, tantalizingly unanswered. And because it leaves so much to the imagination, artists have had a field day. I collect pictures of the annunciation and among my 300+ examples there is almost no artistic stone left unturned. Gabriel usually comes on Mary's right, our left, but there the similarity stops. He stands, he kneels; he commands, he beseeches, he cajoles; he leans towards Mary, he pulls back from her. He is in such a hurry to make his announcement that he is still half way down from the ceiling when speaking, he is composed and kneeling gracefully in front of her; he is tranquil, he is flustered; he whispers, he declaims, he shouts, he wags his finger at her. And Mary kneels calmly and serenely as though this happens every day or she pulls back in fright. Sometimes Gabriel looms over her and she is overwhelmed, in other images she stands stolidly whilst Gabriel pleads. There's something of the ballerina about both of them in many pictures as they dance around each other. In one picture her cat has a fit, in another the cat looks on rather curiously. She is frightened, she scowls, she smiles knowingly, she is impassive. In one modern picture a tiny angel is trying to climb up Mary's tree trunk of a neck to whisper in her ear. One of the most poignant pictures comes from the unlikely source of Andy Warhol whose understated painting simply shows Gabriel's raised hand on the left of the picture and Mary's tense fingers pulling back on her prie-dieu on the right-hand side. One of my favourites is Braccesco's painting in the Louvre, in which Gabriel zooms in from top right on what can only be described as a fifteenth-century surfboard and Mary, quite reasonably, ducks as he heads straight for her head at full tilt.[26]

If poetry is too difficult, try prose. Retell as biblical story through the eyes of one of the characters – perhaps one of the men who lowered their friend through the roof to Jesus, or Ebed-Melech when he found Jeremiah in the pit. Here are two very different ways into the story in Acts 8.26–40 that engage with the biblical story through the eyes of two different people. They may seem slightly long as an introduction but the church concerned expected 30-minute sermons. Note that neither are in the first person – one in the second and one in the third – and so are free to take the role of observer, which is frequently a more creative perspective.

It is almost time to leave. It's been a successful trip: you combined business as a treasury official with pleasure. Now there's just time for a quick dash to buy last-minute souvenirs and something to read on the way home. Better still, a local religious best-seller which can remind you of the visit. Then it's time to take your seat so the long journey can start.

Once you have watched the city disappear into the distance, it is time to settle down and read. There is nothing to watch in the way of scenery so you can give your undivided attention to reading. Good thing you thought to get a book.

But there's a problem. Not with the travel arrangements: no one can complain about personal transport provided by your royal employer. The problem is with the book you grabbed off the shelves. It's a local classic – a few hundred years old to be sure, but everyone still talks about it and it made some sense when you heard it read in their place of worship. But now . . . It's tough to admit that you, who can do all the financial wheeler-dealing necessary to keep the queen happy and have never been defeated by the logic necessary to keep the books of a whole country straight, can't make sense of what this poet is on about. Not only is there no one to ask about it, but there won't be for a long time because all the people who know about it are back in the city, and you are going in the opposite direction through the middle of nowhere. And worse still, you haven't got anything else to read: for the next few days it's this or nothing. Nothing but boredom . . .

There are moments in the Bible stories that I wish were explained in more detail. I would love to know just how

72

Philip knew that he had to get up and take a quick trip down the desert road to Gaza. It was not exactly an everyday sort of thing to do, like nipping out to the shops or to fill up the car: the sort of thing you can do and nobody takes any notice. This involved a deliberate journey into the wilderness for no apparent purpose. What would he say to people he met on the way? 'Where are you off to Philip?' 'O, just a quick trip to the wilderness. City life is getting a bit crowded these days. Suddenly felt like seeing if there was anyone there or if any trees had grown since last time I was there.' 'Are you mad . . .?'

How could he be sure that this was not some wild figment of his imagination? Did he know why he was going? – the Bible suggests he did not. What was the chance of meeting anyone to travel with? – pretty low, and you didn't just enter the wilderness alone. –

We don't know the answers to these questions, but we can be certain that Philip must have pinched himself to see if this was for real. Was he really just getting up and setting off, leaving his four daughters without explanation except that God had called him. Who was Philip, anyway? Someone given to wild ideas and crazy action? No, anything but: the early Christians chose him to serve widows at the daily distribution of food. So he was reliable and good with people, not given to flights of independent fancy. He was of good standing in the community, full of the Spirit and of wisdom, full of faith and the Holy Spirit. He was the last person we would expect to do anything impetuous or to let the widows down by taking off at short notice into the desert. He would not be one to listen to voices in his head, but would apply his God-given wisdom and act accordingly. But, when God called, this steady, reliable pillar of the local church went off to the wilderness road not knowing why, only convinced that God would make it clear sooner or later.

But, think about it: was it so out of character for someone who was full of faith and who could trust that God was not leading him down the garden path. There must be a reason for this odd command to set out on the wilderness road, and he could trust God to make it clear.

And we know the reason. There was an Ethiopian government official who had just set out on the road too in his chariot, his time in Jerusalem over. He had been worshipping God and was studying a scroll of the Scriptures on the way home. He needed to have this explained, and Philip was the one to do it. With hindsight, and knowing the end of the story, we can see that this all makes perfect sense – but we don't live our lives with the benefit of hindsight. For us, as for Philip, the challenge is what do we do in the middle of daily life when there is no hindsight to affirm our action and it seems we are being called to do something either unusual or too demanding. Where, then, is our faith in God? How can we be sure we are hearing God correctly, and not our own ideas?

Having let our imagination loose on Scripture and on the world in which we live, we need to let the two come together in our preaching. On the one hand, we do not want to lose our imaginative streak when tackling the process of writing the sermon, on the other, we have to learn to turn our ideas into words – too many words and we drown the images in verbosity; too few and people don't grasp it. In the middle there is a way to clothe what our imagination has opened up in apposite and fine words that bring our hearers alongside us so they catch our wonder too. Why do we do this? Because we want to throw open some windows on God's grace, rather than close doors.

Notes

1 Ronald Blythe, *Borderland*, Black Dog Books, Norwich, 2005, pp. 120–1.

2 Dr Ruth Etchells, during a night-time pilgrimage in the Cathedral.

3 'A Path in the Woods', in Grażnya Drabik and David Curzon (ed. and trans.), *Astonishments: Selected Poems of Anna Kamieńska*, Paraclete Press, Brewster, MA, 2007.

4 Michel Quoist, *Prayers of Life*, Gill & Macmillan, London, 1965, p. 14.

5 Walter Brueggemann, *Finally Comes the Poet*, Augsburg Fortress, Minneapolis, 1989, p. 109; and Walter Brueggemann, *The Word Militant: Preaching a Decentering Word*, Fortress, Minneapolis, 2007, p. 27.

6 Brueggemann, *Finally Comes the Poet*, pp. 7–11.

7 Walter Brueggemann, *Hopeful Imagination: Prophetic Voices in Exile*, Fortress Press, Philadelphia, 1986, p. 25.

8 David Brown, *Tradition and Imagination*, Oxford University Press, Oxford, 2000, p. 40.

9 Donald Coggan, *Stewards of Grace*, Hodder & Stoughton, London, 1958, pp. 22–3.

10 Andrew Motion, *Guardian* Review Section, 6 October 2007, p. 3.

11 Seamus Heaney, *The Redress of Poetry*, Faber & Faber, London, 1995, pp. 113ff., 141.

12 Ronald Blythe's 'Word from Wormingford' column in the *Church Times* is an example of writing that not only uses words skilfully but also engages people in the world he is describing.

13 Kathleen Norris, 'The New ICEL Psalter', *Cross Currents*, Spring 1996.

14 Timothy Radcliffe, *Why go to Church?* Continuum, London, 2008, p. 46.

15 See http://www.poetrytranslation.org/translation_process/single/About_the_translation_process, accessed 18 August 2008.

16 Macrina Wiederkehr, *A Tree Full of Angels*, Harper & Row, San Francisco, 1988, pp. 145–6.

17 The names of patients have been changed.

18 Copyright © Rosalind Brown 1998.

19 Copyright © Rosalind Brown 1999.

20 In traditional form the sequence is lines of 2 syllables; 4 syllables; 6 syllables; 8 syllables; 2 syllables.

21 Thomas Troeger, *Imagining a Sermon*, Abingdon Press, Nashville, 1990, p. 57.

22 The Collect is that for the Tuesday in Holy Week in the Episcopal Church of the USA.

23 Copyright © Rosalind Brown 1992, 1997.

24 The presence of the ox and donkey around the crib derives from Isaiah 1.3 'The ox knows his owner and the donkey its master's crib', which is taken as a prophetic Scripture. The presence of the animals

thus demonstrates the divinity of the newborn baby, which, as proph-
esied, they recognize.

25 Copyright © Rosalind Brown 1997.

26 Durham Cathedral Sermons:, 'The Annunciation', 18 December
2005, Canon Rosalind Brown.

6

WORSHIP AND WORD

The Foundations of Preaching

Liturgy

'It was Bach's job as Cantor at the St Thomas School of Leipzig to be a musical preacher for the city's main churches.' There is good reason to suppose Bach regarded the primary purpose of cantatas as proclamation of the gospel. It is often forgotten that both the St Matthew Passion and the St John Passion were designed for a preaching service (vespers), the sermon coming during the interval of these works. The passion setting itself would be understood as a form of preaching – the music intensifying the verbal message, enabling the congregation to appropriate the saving power of the gospel story for themselves as they were drawn to the central figure in the drama, Jesus Christ.[1]

With these words, Jeremy Begbie reminds us that all preaching is in the context of worship and the liturgy is part of the proclamation. Liturgy is, literally, the work of the people, and preachers can let the liturgy do its work since, perhaps more than the sermon itself, it brings people close to God. Liturgy doesn't tell people what to do, it enables them to do it. By offering eloquent and apposite words, it raises and develops themes that the sermon can pick up long before and long after the preacher has entered the pulpit and it allows the people of God to respond to the proclamation of the kingdom of God. William Temple said that it is the worshipping life that will transform the world,[2] and if we preach without regard to liturgy the work of the people is cramped or – worse – belittled by our lack of attention to their part in the corporate worship; it suggests we have forgotten that preaching is a congregational activity that continues beyond the church door, not just something the preacher does to them in church.

Even so-called non-liturgical churches have a liturgical structure in their worship which the preacher needs to understand. A funeral I attended in an African-American Pentecostal church was more liturgically precise than many an Anglican service and the preacher knew exactly what ground he had to cover and how he was to do so. The familiarity of liturgy is helpful to children, many elderly people and also to some people with learning difficulties or autism. Children know the routine of liturgy: when giving a children's talk in a colleague's parish I was interrupted by his son, who announced in a loud voice, 'You're not doing it properly like my Daddy does it' and proceeded to tell me exactly how to phrase my questions!

Perhaps more important than the precise words of the liturgy is its overall structure. Liturgy breathes, it has a rhythm, it ebbs and flows. Liturgy both holds and moves the people forward, providing them with the security of familiar words and actions while creating room for the Holy Spirit to breathe new life, not least through the sermon. The preacher who respects the integrity of liturgy by working within this given context enables a liturgical sermon to be part of the liturgy rather than an interruption to it, to be itself an act of worship. This affects not only the choice of theme but the language used which should not draw attention to itself by being either old fashioned or the latest language from the street, but should be consonant with both the liturgy and the concerns of the world beyond the church door. Liturgy provides a multi-sensory environment for the sermon – good liturgy embodies sight, sound, space and smell. The liturgical colours set the visual scene (has anyone explained them to the congregation?) and there is a rhythm of participation for the congregation as they both act and receive.

The weekly Collects are available as liturgical preaching resources; the Church's prayer for the week can act as a helpful filter for the Scriptures, and the liturgical year can suggest themes for the sermon. For example, hope and judgement may influence the interpretation of readings in Advent, as may revelation in Epiphany or testing and discipleship in Lent. This influence is classically illustrated by the lectionary's setting of the story of the transfiguration: a preacher with this text on the Sunday before Lent may nuance it by looking back to Epiphany's theme or forward to Lent's; faced with the same text on the Feast of the Transfiguration, a sermon may let the story stand on its own or take account of the paradox that this is Hiroshima Day, while a midweek homily based on the course reading of a Gospel will set it in the context of that particular Gospel's overall story. To return to Psalm 137, a text that is rarely prayed or preached in its entirety, out of the lectionary's caution, a sermon preached on it in Advent, when the defiant yearning of the exiles might be a focus, would be different from one at a choir festival when the role of song in keeping faith alive could be considered, or in Christian Aid Week when the last verses could be used to explore how we respond to the horrific legacy of war (a challenging sermon to prepare!).

In liturgical preaching the Scriptures are read, heard and interpreted in the context of a community of faith gathered to worship God and be transformed and renewed. For Anglicans the principal context shifted from Matins to the Eucharist in the twentieth century and the sermon moved from being the conclusion of a service of the Word to part of a service of Word and Sacrament. At Matins or Evensong, this concluding position of the sermon needs to be considered, as does the relationship to the Psalms and Canticles, which give us access not only to the actions but to the words and prayers of our forebears in the faith and may themselves be the inspiration for the sermon.[3] The sermon should not be an anti-climax to the worship, which does not mean homiletic fireworks but a sermon that draws together what has gone before and sends people out with a sense of how their worship can be transformative. Sensitivity to the relationship that has been built up between the congregation, the person leading the service and the building is always important: for example, a highly interactive sermon using multi-media techniques might disturb what the previous hour has established.

The Eucharist is a very different context for preaching. If preaching is proclamation in words, then, in Paul's thought, what happens at the table is proclamation through liturgical action, 'For as often as you eat this bread and drink the cup, you proclaim the Lord's death until he comes' (1 Corinthians 11.26). The two are part of the same proclamation of the word and must be univocal. This service does not build towards a single point but, book-ended by the important gathering and dismissal, has two foci that reflect the structural division of the service into word and sacrament. The first action of the people and priest in eucharistic worship, the greeting 'The Lord be with you / And also with you', is repeated without fanfare at the beginning of the Liturgy of the Sacrament; these two brief greetings establish the relationship of president and people together before God and it is rarely appropriate for the preacher to greet the people again from the pulpit.

The structure of the Holy Eucharist is clear if we write out the headings and subheadings in *Common Worship*.[4] Liturgies of most other churches have similar structures that echo the liturgical texts of the early Church. There is movement in the liturgy and the sermon has to move in that direction, not act as a roadblock or diversion from which people have to regroup and restart the journey. The sermon is neither a freestanding event nor the climax of the service, so it must honour its context and not upstage the Eucharist that follows. Instead, the flowing movement within the structure reaches towards a high point within each part – the sermon and the Eucharist. In *Common Worship* it is part of the fourth action of the people and the priest (note the order) to 'proclaim and respond to the word of God' which comprises hearing the Scriptures, singing a psalm, canticle or hymn, the sermon and the congregation's affirmation of faith and finally the intercessions.[5] *Common Worship* gives scope for some flexibility in the form of the sermon[6] but the style of preaching still needs to honour the essentially lyrical language of the liturgy rather than adopt less poetic forms like points and propositions which belong in the lecture hall. Less formal approaches need careful thought about the particular circumstances of this service in this church on this occasion.

If liturgy is the context of preaching, Scripture is its catalyst and our key dialogue partner. Kevin Irwin reminds us that in and through the liturgy the word is always contemporary and the written word of the Bible returns to its native context when it is proclaimed liturgically in the hearing of believers. The liturgy preserves the communal nature of hearing and responding to the Scriptures.[7] The preacher can facilitate this communal response to the Scriptures, relating them to the congregation's life in the Church and world, as well as to the rest of the liturgy, creating the space for the Holy Spirit to breathe new life through it in the worship. In this liturgical environment the possibility of transformation is a given: the saving events of the past become possibilities for us and we respond to them, notably in hymnody, which can give voice to people's yearnings and delights and should be taken into account so that they function properly in relation to the sermon. Preachers should be aware of how hymns can press home the sermon's theme or shed further creative light on it through their embodiment of poetry set to music rather than prose, and perhaps refer to a line or two as an aide-memoire for the congregation.[8]

So what are we doing when we preach in the liturgy? Here is one explanation,

> Our purpose is to plunge our listeners and ourselves into an experience of God, an experience which will naturally lead to a celebration which seeps into our bones and urges us toward change. Homiletic preaching is directed to deeper and deeper conversion of already faithful believers.[9]

If that is our intent, not only should we preach with the conviction that the sermon can be effective through the work of the Holy Spirit in growth in holiness, but our conclusion should lead people seamlessly back into the overall liturgy so that they can stand before God in the light of what they have heard. A time of silence at the end of the sermon enables people to reflect on what they have heard and to prepare themselves to respond in the rest of the liturgy. Most immediately there is our common confession of faith in the creed, prayers for the world, and the eucharistic celebration which catches us up in the mystery of Christ's presence with us through the sacrament. Then there is the dismissal and the living of transformed lives in the world for which the church has prayed. That perspective beyond the church doors always needs a place in our preaching.

Biblical preaching

At ordination, the only thing given to a new deacon or priest is the Bible. Faithful preaching takes both the Bible and life today seriously. The veteran preacher John Stott prayed for preachers 'who refuse to sacrifice truth to relevance or relevance to truth, but who resolve in equal measure to be faithful to Scripture and pertinent to today'.[10] Scripture is foundational to preaching, but biblical preaching does not mean simply quoting the Bible: Leander Keck decries preaching that quotes a verse from Scripture and goes on to say something that could have been suggested just as well by a fortune cookie.[11] A sermon may be profoundly biblical without any direct quotation because it aims to draw people irresistibly into the world of Scripture so they can live there for themselves.

How do we interact with Scripture in our preaching? Academic study is essential and should not stop when pre-ordination training ends. Two opposite dangers are to inhabit the world of the past or to ignore it. Franz Kampaus criticizes attempts to lead people back into the past by describing its situation to them but then leaving them in an alien world into which we unconsciously read contemporary attitudes. He argues that,

The proclamation of the Christian message in the gospels points in the opposite direction. Certainly it remains firmly rooted in the history of Jesus. But it presses forward, as it were, with this history to support it from behind, in the awareness of the presence of the Lord, in order to become engaged in the new set of circumstances before it.[12]

John Stott calls this first approach antiquarianism, but points to the opposite danger of avoiding the discipline of discovering what the text meant in the first place by rushing to the message for today. This is surrendering to existentialism unrelated to past revelation. Instead he advocates that we aim to bring the past and the present together.[13]

One approach is expository preaching, which aims to make biblical truth intelligible to the hearers as the preacher takes the role of interpreter, standing between the text and the hearers. This approach works through a text closely, letting it set the agenda, although it is best avoided for parables and poetry that do not respond well to dissection into very small sections. This approach builds up people's knowledge of the Bible, although they hear and interpret Scripture through the preacher, whereas in a Bible study or discussion group, rather than be taught, they can explore the Scriptures for themselves and conversation can occur. While this approach emphasizes the importance of Scripture, McClure's concern is that it can narrow a preacher's engagement with culture or human experience and promotes a utilitarian or pragmatic approach to the Bible that must always be applied to daily life.[14] Encouraging the congregation to follow the sermon in their Bibles also sends a message that preaching is about textual understanding rather than mutual encounter with God's word because it keeps everyone's eyes down and makes eye contact between the preacher and the congregation impossible.

At the other extreme some people, like Lowry, begin from the present world of the hearers, choosing and marshalling Scripture readings to help with problem-solving in the hearers' lives. Passages may be synthesized and applied to the controlling theme of the sermon with the aim of informing people about an aspect of Christian belief apposite to their needs and moving them to relevant action. While this can yield interesting sermons, it can also become very parochial and will not help people to enter and grasp the overall shape of the biblical world. A further variation on this is to have a sermon series that follows a theme.[15] My preference is to begin from Scripture when preparing a sermon;[16] we may say much the same thing as we would have said had we started from an issue and brought Scripture to bear on it, but the emphasis is different and by beginning in Scripture we model its place in our own lives.[17]

Lectionary preaching

The wide adoption of the lectionary facilitates a different pattern of engagement with Scripture.[18] Congregations hear two or three readings, including a course reading of a Gospel, giving scope for more holistic understanding of the Bible as it is in dialogue with itself. A clever observation reminds us of the challenge this may present the preacher, 'The law of Moses and the Book of Proverbs say that if we are good workers, help the poor, and keep away from strange women, God will bless us and prosper us. Job and the Psalms say, we are, and we did, and we have, and he hasn't!'[19] The initial decision facing the preacher is whether to preach from one or a combination of the readings, including the Psalms and Canticles. If the Gospel is chosen the sermon becomes part of an ongoing exploration of the life of Jesus Christ as described in the Gospel for that year. If the Old or New Testament reading is the focus for the sermon, the congregation's exposure to the whole biblical canon is expanded.[20]

Preaching from the Old Testament raises the question of whether it should normally be interpreted through the lens of the New Testament. There are times when it is appropriate to preach from the Old Testament Christologically, but it has its own integrity and we should not silence its voices that speak to us from the centuries before the incarnation. Frederick Robertson, preaching on Job's words, 'I know that my Redeemer liveth', explained how to honour both the Old Testament context and our faith as Christians:

> We must not throw into these words of Job a meaning which Job had not . . . Job was an Arabian Emir not a Christian. All that Job meant by these words was that he knew he had a vindicator in God . . . But God has given to us, for our faith to rest on, something more distinct and tangible than he gave to Job . . . It is all this added meaning gained from Christ with which we use these words, 'I know that my Redeemer liveth'. But we must remember that all was not revealed to Job.[21]

The classic example is Isaiah 7.14, to which Matthew gave the familiar Christological interpretation, yet there is a very different sermon to be preached if it is left in its original context of Ahaz's refusal of a sign when under threat of attack: when I did preach about that I could see eyes almost popping at the realization the text was not originally a prophecy of the birth of Christ.[22] Gerhard von Rad, the great twentieth-century Old Testament scholar, caught the wonder of this polyvalence of Scripture when he wrote that what seems to be the fulfilment of God's word in one context 'gives rise, all unexpected, to the promise of yet greater things. Here nothing carries ultimate meaning in itself, but is ever the earnest of yet greater wonders.'[23] We can revel in the rich resources for preaching the Old Testament in its own right – the wonderful narratives, the fraught history, the urgency of the prophets, the horror of judgement, the glory of restoration, the vibrancy of prayers and the measured perception of the wisdom literature – as well as seeing in it depths that were not known in its original context. The decision whether or not to preach Old Testament texts Christologically may therefore vary from week to week.[24]

The lectionary opens up a still more challenging but frequently more rewarding approach: to let the Scriptures interact with each other so that a sermon emerges from within that interaction. This approach requires more concentrated preparation because time and space have to be allowed for them to bounce off and nuance each other. The juxtaposition of the wider biblical record with a particular passage of Scripture may enhance our insight or jolt us to attention and potentially add piquancy to the sermon. The congregation is exposed to the expansiveness of Scripture and invited to explore its bigger picture for themselves.[25]

With lectionary preaching, whether the preacher starts from one Scripture or from two or three, Scripture provides the framework for the sermon, although it does not necessarily set the final agenda as in an exegetical sermon. Preparatory exploration of Scripture and prayerful consideration of the needs of the congregation might suggest a particular sermon focus to which the Scriptures make the fundamental contribution as frame rather than theme.[26] This interaction with all the readings and with the contemporary life of the congregation and world makes for exciting sermon preparation since never again will these particular elements combine in this way – next time the readings are set, daily life will be different and a different sermon will emerge.

If we become experienced in beginning from Scripture in this way, we will find that when a crisis occurs which we cannot ignore when preaching (9/11 and the death of the Princess of Wales being two examples), we do not have to look for other Scriptures but know how to begin from the lectionary readings and let them shape a sermon which remains rooted in the stability of the weekly liturgy and keeps the focus on God while doing justice to the crisis. That stability is, in itself, a pastoral support in a time of disorientation.

Different genres of Scripture

In the early days of the homiletic revolution, Craddock argued that, rather than adopt the same methodology week in, week out, the genre of Scripture should suggest the style of sermon. For Paul Marshall, preaching is biblical when the sermon is determined by the content of the text and when it has the same function as the text.[27] These may be slightly different things and so different genres will suggest different approaches to preaching.

Much of the Bible is narrative or history whose power lies in being a story that the hearers can enter, so to preach about what it means is to miss the point. If we let stories be stories rather than a series of propositions, they will draw us into their world and ask us life-changing questions. As soon as children hear 'Once upon a time' their imaginations are in gear, and preaching can keep that joy alive for adults too (church is just about the only place where adults are read to). Good stories in Scripture are theologically true whether or not they are historically true, but we should heed Long's caution that we must never let other stories erode or replace the overarching gospel story.[28]

The Bible is a book about real people like us and narrative can help us preach on legal and ethical material by fleshing it out with stories from life. So, when preaching on the Ten Commandments, why not tell the stories of David and Bathsheba or Ahab taking Naboth's vineyard to show what happens when you covet your neighbour's wife or livelihood? When we need to illustrate the laws about how the nation was to welcome the orphan and the widow (think refugees and economic migrants), there is the story of Ruth and Naomi; and if not bearing false witness against your neighbour needs fleshing out, there is the story of Susanna in the Apocrypha. This approach can also be adopted with the epistles, using invented stories if biblical ones are not available.[29]

The prophets spoke God's message as mouthpieces, messengers or ambassadors. They proclaimed it faithfully without embellishment or gloss, frequently in condemnation of the nation's way of life. This style of preaching is one from which many preachers shy away today, perhaps because we fear being thought judgemental. But preaching from the prophets is called for at times and is not foretelling the future but see-ing the world in the light of God's promises; preaching both God's judgement and God's redemption, which in the gospel belong gloriously together. The effect can be vivid: from John the Baptist's 'you brood of vipers' to Hosea's picture of God as a parent teaching a child to walk, or Jesus as a mother hen gathering her wayward chicks.

When preaching from wisdom literature, it can be helpful to adopt the approach of 'let's think about this together in our own context' and to explore the implications of pithy sayings that trip off the tongue too fast to take them all in. The Dean of Durham set a passage from Proverbs about wisdom in the context of the return of students for a new academic year, while on another occasion the difference between wisdom and knowledge in our contemporary society was explored in rela-tion to a narrative passage of Scripture.[30]

The poetic literature opens up many preaching possibilities. The Psalms are the vibrant prayers of people who had robust relationships with God and were not afraid to express them-selves forthrightly, with exaltation beyond our greatest hymns of today, and lament or anger that never finds its way into our prayers, at least in public. There is the sexual poetry of the Song of Solomon and the devastation of Lamentations as the desolation of the city is painted for us in words that singe us almost as painfully as the fires that burned Jerusalem. The possibilities for preaching these poetic writings are wide,[31] but remember that poetry is evocative and open-ended and its power can be drained by pedantic explanation. It is wise to help people engage with the genre for themselves as well as to exegete a particular example or preach about the context from which the poetry emerged.[32] However we preach poetic litera-ture, it is important to understand the principles of Hebrew poetry: put very simply, what makes a poem a poem in Hebrew is not rhyming words but parallelism which says something once then says it again slightly differently – 'Comfort, O comfort my people says your God / Speak tenderly to Jerusalem and cry to her that she has served her term' (Isaiah 40.1) or uses repetition or refrains (Psalms 118; 136). Simply explaining parallelism to a congregation that says the Psalms regularly can open up new horizons for them.

The parables are patently not historically true, but in Jesus' hands were stunning illustrations which caught the hearers out. Think of the times the religious leaders found themselves suddenly uncomfortably aware that Jesus had told a good story and the punchline was against them. They didn't need to have the meaning explained, it was all too horribly clear. Parables master us, we can't master them so explaining their meaning is guaranteed to suck all the power out of the story (although we may have to help people understand the cultural assumptions of the parable).[33] Another mistake made when preaching parables is to ignore their original purpose: if Jesus began a parable by saying 'the kingdom of heaven will be like this . . .' then he meant it to be eschatological and corporate and not (as I once heard preached) an appeal for personal devotion. Allegorical interpretation of parables, which introduces far too many confusing aspects into focused stories, fell out of favour centuries ago and should be left for dead.

The epistles were written to particular churches at particular times for particular purposes and we abuse them with vast generalizations from short extracts. It is better to help the congregation to understand the situation facing the original congregation – exegete that congregation to this congregation – so that they can experience the impact of hearing the words for the first time. We will never know why Euodia and Syntyche fell out (Philippians 4.2) but we all know the tension of being in a room with two people at daggers drawn, so let people feel the impact of Paul addressing what was perhaps the first big loss of fellowship in that church and hear his demand, 'help these women'. The letters to the Thessalonians were about vibrant issues arising from the expectation that the Lord was coming soon. Put the congregation's feet in those shoes – the sheer anticipation and hope into which that letter was written – and imagine the sensation when the 'spiritual' people who had given up work to wait for Christ's coming heard Paul tell them to get off their bottoms and get a job, or the joy of those who had their fears assuaged about their recently dead relatives missing the resurrection. Only then consider the practical advice Paul gave about how they should live in the interim (1 Thessalonians 4.13—5.11; 2 Thessalonians 3.6–13).

Whatever genre of Scripture we are working with, it is vital that we not only honour the genre but also honour the Scripture as the foundation of the sermon. Our imaginations should be given free reign in the early stages of preparation alongside study of the passage, but they can lead us astray if we are not ruthless with our more exotic musings once we begin to shape the sermon. Otherwise we will end up doing *eisegesis* (reading things into the text) rather than *exegesis* (reading things from the text) and will abuse the text by treating it as a trampoline from which to bounce off in all directions.

Our exposure to Scripture

A review of a book on the Psalms refers to 'the beauty of the exposition of the scriptures in Christian preaching'.[34] Beauty is our aim but a sermon is only as vital and beautiful as our engagement with Scripture is vibrant; preaching requires our commitment to regular and deep engagement with God's word in devotional reading and study. That, more than anything, is what the congregation will notice in our preaching: immersion in, not ingenuity with, God's word. If our reading of the Bible is being skimped, an urgent review is needed because our homiletic lifeblood is ceasing to pump through our body. We begin with our own exposure to Scripture, letting it, as Barbara Brown Taylor graphically puts it, read us rather than us read it:

I cannot think of any other text [than the Bible] that has such authority over me, interpreting me faster than I can interpret it. It speaks to me not with the stuffy voice of some mummified sage but with the fresh, lively voice of someone who knows what happened to me an hour ago. Familiar passages accumulate meaning as I return to them again and again. They seem to grow during my absences from them; I am always finding something new in them that I never discovered before, something designed to meet me where I am at this particular moment in time.[35]

As preachers, the best gift we can give our hearers is an example of passion for God's word and for worship.

Notes

1 Jeremy Begbie, *Resounding Truth: Christian Wisdom in the World of Music*, SPCK, London, 2008, p. 123, quoting Michael Marissen.

2 Quoted in Geoffrey Rowell, Kenneth Stevenson and Rowan Williams (eds), *Love's Redeeming Work: The Anglican Quest for Holiness*, Oxford University Press, Oxford, 2001, p. 581.

3 Durham Cathedral Sermons: 17 December 2006, 'Based on St Luke 1:68', Canon David Kennedy; 24 February 2008, 'Expectans Expectavi', Canon David Kennedy.

4 *Common Worship*, Church House Publishing, London, 2000. The discussion here relates to pp. 166ff. The structure can be identified from the headings printed in large red italics in *Common Worship*. Within them the various components of the liturgy are identified by black headings that are right-hand justified in the book.

5 The prayers of intercession should sit comfortably with the rest of the service including the sermon, since they are part of the congregation's response to the worship thus far, which includes the sermon. Liaison between preacher and intercessor is therefore advisable beforehand unless the intercessor is very adept at reshaping prepared prayers in the light of the preaching. If the preacher is leading the prayers, they should be planned to include some petitions that facilitate congregational response and should not merely repeat the sermon in prayer form.

6 'The sermon is an integral part of the Liturgy of the Word . . . [It] may on occasion include less formal exposition of Scripture, the

use of drama, interviews, discussion and audio visual aids.' *Common Worship*, p. 332.

7 Kevin Irwin, *Context and Text: Method in Liturgical Theology*, Pueblo, Collegeville, MN, 1994, pp. 86–90.

8 See Rosalind Brown, *How Hymns Shape our Lives*, Grove Books, Cambridge, 2001.

9 Mary Ann Wiesemann-Mills, *Preaching in the Context of 'Doing the Liturgy'*, in Michael Monshau (ed.), *Preaching at the Double Feast: Homiletics for Eucharistic Worship*, Liturgical Press, Collegeville, MN, 2006, p. 151.

10 John Stott, *Between Two Worlds: The Art of Preaching in the Twentieth Century*, Eerdmans, Grand Rapids, 1982, p. 144 (also published as *I Believe in Preaching*, Hodder & Stoughton, London, 1982).

11 Leander E. Keck, *The Bible in the Pulpit*, Abingdon Press, Nashville, 1978, p. 101.

12 Franz Kampaus, *The Gospels for Preachers and Teachers*, Sheed & Ward, London, 1968, p. 351.

13 John Stott, 'Biblical Preaching in the Modern World', in Michael P. Knowles (ed.), *The Folly of Preaching: Models and Methods*, Eerdmans, Grand Rapids, 2007, p. 124.

14 John S. McClure, *Preaching Words: 144 Key Terms in Homiletics*, Westminster John Knox, Louisville, 2007, p. 31.

15 See Phillip Tovey, *Preaching a Sermon Series with Common Worship*, Grove Books Worship Series, Cambridge, 2004, for ideas on this. In Lent 2009 Durham Cathedral housed a sculpture exhibition, *On Being Human*, and adopted that theme for its Lent Course, and some sermons also engaged with that theme. See Durham Cathedral Sermons: 1 March 2009, 'Stories about Being Human', Canon Rosalind Brown; 15 March 2009, 'Bom Boys in Egypt', The Very Revd Michael Sadgrove; 22 March 2009, 'Apartheid of the Mind', Canon Stephen Cherry; 29 March 2009, 'Rivers Run Through It', Canon Rosalind Brown.

16 That does not mean we open the sermon itself with a biblical quotation, but our preparation has begun from Scripture.

17 For example, Durham Cathedral Sermons: 18 January 2009, 'Visions and Realities', Canon Rosalind Brown, could have begun from the American inauguration or the tragedy in Gaza, but I chose to begin from the Scripture and to weave world events into that context.

18 For more information on how the lectionary is constructed see Gordon Giles, 'The Sunday Lectionary', in Paul Bradshaw (ed.), *Companion to Common Worship*, vol. i, SPCK, London, 2001, pp. 225ff. and Anne Dawtry, 'The Weekday Lectionary', in Paul Bradshaw (ed.), *A Companion to Common Worship*, vol. ii, SPCK, London, 2006, pp. 33–49.

19 Quoted in *News of Hymnody*, date not recorded, and attributed to OT theologians at St John's College, Nottingham.

20 Durham Cathedral Sermons: 12 February 2008, 'On not Settling for Knowledge Alone', Canon Rosalind Brown; 20 April 2008, 'Easter, Death and Life', Canon Rosalind Brown; 22 June 2008 'David', Canon Rosalind Brown.

21 Frederick W. Robertson, 'Realising the Second Advent', in *Sermons Preached at Brighton*, Henry S. King and Co., London, 1872, p. 151.

22 Durham Cathedral Sermons: 23 December 2007, 'Tested by God's Word and God's Silence', Canon Rosalind Brown.

23 Gerhard von Rad, 'Typological Interpretation of the Old Testament', in Claus Westermann (ed.), *Essays on Old Testament Hermeneutics*, John Knox Press, Atlanta, 1963, p. 34.

24 Durham Cathedral Sermons: 9 April 2006, 'Vineyards', Canon Rosalind Brown; 30 July 2006, 'Job', Canon Rosalind Brown; 11 March 2007, 'Deceiving Jacob', Canon Rosalind Brown; 22 June 2008, 'David', Canon Rosalind Brown; 9 December 2007, 'Showdown at Mount Carmel', Canon David Kennedy; 1 June 2008, 'Two Sermons on Friendship: Ruth and Naomi', The Very Revd Michael Sadgrove; 8 June 2008, 'Two Sermons on Friendship: David and Jonathan', The Very Revd Michael Sadgrove; 5 April 2009, 'Rivers Run Through It', Canon Rosalind Brown.

25 Durham Cathedral Sermons: 18 November 2007, 'Daniel and the Parable of the Sower', Canon Rosalind Brown; 27 July 2008, 'Angels in Confined Spaces', Canon Rosalind Brown.

26 Durham Cathedral Sermons: 24 November 2007, 'Christ the King', Canon Rosalind Brown; 20 January 2008, 'Our Baptismal Calling', Canon Rosalind Brown; 17 August 2008, 'Hospitality', Canon Rosalind Brown; 24 August 2008, 'Following Bartholomew's Example', Canon Rosalind Brown; 31 August 2008, 'St Aidan', Canon Rosalind Brown; 7 September 2008, 'Cuthbert and Benedict', Canon Rosalind Brown.

27 Paul Marshall, *Preaching for the Church Today*, Church Hymnal Corporation, New York, 1990, p. 73.

28 Thomas Long, *The Witness of Preaching*, Westminster John Knox, Louisville, 1989, p. 41.

29 Durham Cathedral Sermons: 11 January 2009, 'Little Trespass: Big Guilt', Canon Ian Jagger.

30 Durham Cathedral Sermons: 5 October 2008, 'On Volvo Sunday', The Very Revd Michael Sadgrove; 10 February 2008, 'On Not Settling for Knowledge Alone', Canon Rosalind Brown.

31 Durham Cathedral Sermons: 25 June 2005, 'Singing the Lord's Song', The Very Revd Michael Sadgrove; 2 September 2007, 'Psalm

119 and St Benedict', Canon David Kennedy; 9 March 2008, 'Lamentations', Canon Rosalind Brown.

32 Durham Cathedral Sermons: 24 December 2006, 'Psalm 85.10', Canon David Kennedy; 18 May 2008, 'Holy, Holy, Holy', Canon David Kennedy; 4 May 2008, 'The Choral Offices of the Church', The Very Revd Michael Sadgrove.

33 Durham Cathedral Sermons: 12 October 2008, 'Matthew's Wedding Feast', The Venerable Ian Jagger.

34 O. C. Edwards, Jr, reviewing Jason Byassee, *Praise Seeking Understanding: Reading the Psalms with Augustine*, in the *Anglican Theological Review* 9.1 (Winter 2009), p. 146.

35 Barbara Brown Taylor, *The Preaching Life*, Cowley, Cambridge, MA, 1993, p. 52.

7

PASTORAL AND PROPHETIC

The Focuses of Preaching

Faithful preaching comes from a pastoral heart and embodies a prophetic message. We offer pastoral care in our preaching and will reach many people at one time within the context of worship. This gives a sense of proportion that is missing when the focus is entirely on an individual's problem. Pastoral preaching rests on knowing our hearers, who soon realize whether or not we understand and care for them as individuals and as a congregation. Paul Bull berated preachers who preach to the absent or – worse – to themselves and described how, when newly ordained, he preached an eloquent series of sermons on the existence of God to a congregation of old ladies who had never for a moment doubted it.[1]

Knowing the congregation

In any congregation there will be people who want to be helped to come to faith and others who hope to have their faith deepened; some will need teaching or persuading, others comforting or converting; some want comfort in distress and others want direction for the future. People come to church at all stages of faith and human development, and their needs cannot all be met fully at the same time.[2] Centuries ago, Augustine recognized the need to know his congregation and the difference when preaching,

Whether there are few or many; whether learned or unlearned, or a mixed audience of both classes; whether they are towns-folk or country folk, or both together; or a gathering in which all sorts and conditions of [humanity] are represented. For it cannot fail to be the case that different persons should affect in different ways the one who intends to instruct orally and likewise the one who intends to give a formal discourse.[3]

Developing this thought, the same words will be heard differently by an old lady and a teenage boy, an engineer and someone who cannot read. While we cannot control what people do with our words, we can try to ensure we are not misunderstood. Many people are at Stage 3 of Fowler's stages of faith, the conformist phase when they are influenced in their beliefs by the authority of others (including the Bible, which is often interpreted literally) but, even though beliefs are held deeply, they have not been studied objectively. Challenges to unexamined certainties are perceived as threats, which helps to explain the conflicts that arise when preachers do not handle controversial subjects carefully in the pulpit: people dig their heels in, feeling threatened. This stage of faith is associated with adolescence, after the literalness of childhood, but many adults do not move beyond it, and our role as preachers may be to help them to mature in their faith by facing the questions and tensions of faith, when life-events bruise their present faith framework, in a safe yet challenging environment.

In addition to understanding something about people's faith development, congregational studies provide useful resources for anyone wanting to study their local church both within itself and in its context.[4] They help us to understand the corporate nature of the church rather than to define the congregation as a collection of individuals. We can begin simply by being attentive as we listen to and observe people and groups in the church and neighbourhood. It helps to walk around the streets being conscious of the social and cultural contexts, the employment situation, the physical environment in bricks and mortar, the parks and high-rise flats, the transport links, the noise or the tranquillity, the beauty and the ugliness, the isolation or the sociability. How are people affected by their environment? Is it safe on the streets? What do people do all day? Is there a sense of community? Who are the voiceless and neglected people and how can we help them to listen to the good news?[5] Do people experience God in their lives? And, if so, who is God for them? What is the role of the church in people's lives? Is folk religion strong? If people do come to church, is concentration difficult because they have they been kept awake at night by crying babies, shift work or street noise? Do they have any biblical background or will they miss our allusions and references? What does the word 'Easter' mean to them? What are their ways of learning? The best sermon will leave people cold or confused if our preaching style is, for example, highly philosophical while they learn by doing; better to aim to meet our hearers on their ground rather than require them to meet on ours.[6]

Study of the congregation is sometimes called 'exegeting the congregation', to complement 'exegeting the text'. However, Thomas Long cautions against driving a wedge between the two and advocates that the preacher begins by engaging with the Scriptures in a representative way on behalf of the congregation, knowing their hopes and fears, dreams and dreads. The congregation–text encounter that the preacher has had on their behalf can then be carried into the sermon, 'The bridge the preacher must now cross is the one between the text-in-congregational-context and the sermon-in-congregational-context.'[7]

Pastoral preaching

At the heart of many pastoral dilemmas is the question the psalmist raised in the face of exile and loss of identity, 'How could we sing the LORD's song in a foreign land?' (Psalm 137.4). Pastoral and prophetic preaching recognizes the pain of being forced to dwell in a foreign land (often the foreign land of bereavement of one kind or another), holds out hope that there is still a song to sing, and offers ways to find the first note.

Pastoral and prophetic preaching are two sides of one coin. There is always a temptation to collude with the congregation in the name of pastoral care, to tell them what they want to hear in a deeply comforting sermon when the truly pastoral approach may be to include a prophetic edge that both holds out the hope of something different and invites or challenges the hearers to risk reaching for it. Equally, prophetic preaching needs a pastoral edge if people are to receive it. Pastoral preaching frequently emphasizes the truths of the incarnation – that God has taken human flesh and come among us, sharing our life. Prophetic preaching embodies the truths of the resurrection and ascension, that God has raised Christ from the dead and exalted him in glory, thus opening the way to the outpouring of the Holy Spirit at Pentecost. It orientates us towards the possibility of change and new life beyond anything we have ever dreamed possible. Incarnation and redemption belong together in the gospel and they belong together in preaching, otherwise we offer platitudes without hope or dislocation without stability.

Pastoral preaching doesn't just *name* difficult situations, it has something to say *about* the situations and points people to the source of hope and help to face them. Peter Hawkins speaks of 'A vision of a world in which there are more bridges than borders',[8] and the aim of pastoral, prophetic preaching has been described as being to stand 'with one foot firmly planted in the congregation and one foot firmly planted in the larger gospel vision [straddling] the abyss – striving to love and affirm the congregation, while, at the same time, prodding and stretching it toward a larger worldview and greater faithfulness to its own gospel'.[9] Walter Brueggemann has identified three voices that affect preaching, those of the biblical text, the pastor and the congregation. He suggests that often the pastor teams up with the text to 'triangle' against the congregation, leaving them as outsiders, and advocates the better way of pastor and congregation standing against the text, allowing the radical word of God to offend both.[10] However, if the preacher is a long-time member of the local community,[11] the preacher and congregation may side together in resisting the text, restricting or imposing upon it a locally familiar or comfortable interpretation and refusing it the freedom to challenge or breathe new life among them. Hence the importance of the bishop's charge to preach the word out of season, when it is not welcome, as well as in season.

Preaching will never replace pastoral care, but much pastoral work is done through sermons, not least by giving people something that is within their reach to do, a small step that will set them on the longer journey. Even a small congregation gathered in a freezing church on a bleak February day includes people whose pastoral needs, whether clearly articulated or not, affect the way that they hear the sermon and enter into the worship. Some will have come to church specifically because of a pastoral event, for example bereavement or a significant anniversary. Few will tell us, so we are always preaching to unknown pastoral situations and it is one of the mysteries of preaching when people say as they leave church, 'your sermon has helped me' but we have no idea why. Others find their memory jogged while they are in church and are caught unawares by emotions they thought were long since dealt with – we can never tell what memory the most innocuous choice of hymn will trigger for someone.

Every sermon should be checked for how it will sound to someone in distress: can it be misunderstood and is there clear good news in it somewhere? It is pastoral to check if people who are hard of hearing can hear and see us in good light (for lip-reading) and to have copies of sermons available in hard copy or on a website for anyone who hasn't heard clearly or couldn't negotiate the sermon – people with autism have difficulty following changes in direction and, because they think literally and visually, stumble over unnecessary ambiguities ('please take a seat').[12] The pastoral ministry of the sermon can be developed when we hang around and chat after the service.

Bereavement can spark a variety of emotions from profound grief to immense relief and freedom; spiritual turmoil to strengthened faith. Bereavements are not only through death but through job loss, financial problems, ill-health or separation from family and friends. Some of these are more easily acknowledged in public than others – society generally has more sympathy for someone who has lost a close relative than someone who has lost a job, not least because there are familiar rituals that we can fulfil in the case of the former. Other people will be facing significant but not tragic crises: decisions about moving to a new area, a career change, putting an elderly relative in a home. Someone who has come to church brimming with joy and wanting to find a way to express their gratitude to God will sit next to a person being ground down by the relentless demands of life and who is seeking reassurance of God's presence in the midst of the tediously ordinary. Sometimes, pastoral needs affect the community as a whole: a strike; a missing child; a school closure; a spate of unsolved crimes that generate fear; while if a major employer is known to be considering redundancies the person who has to make the decision may be worshipping alongside those who will be affected.[13]

People in any or all of these situations can walk into church and sit in front of us on a Sunday when we preach, hoping to be helped to discover God's presence and purpose in their life. We cannot preach about each and every situation, but we can help people, as they do their work in the liturgy, to find God's presence and help in their daily lives. Too many people only hear a sermon about death at a funeral, about family life on Mothering Sunday, or about stewardship when there is a financial need. In each case the context inevitably skews the content towards one aspect of the much broader themes that ought to be explored from the pulpit.[14] Pastoral preaching means not saving our sermons about pastoral issues for a crisis but preaching about birth and death, baptism and marriage, loss and grief at other appropriate times, thus giving people resources they can use when the need arises.[15] If the first time they have heard us preach on death is at their mother's funeral they will not have the resources in place to face her dying with theologically grounded Christian hope. During my first Easter season in a parish I preached on death and resurrection, and some people expressed surprise to hear that we do not become angels when we die, a revelation that had significant repercussions for the way they (reflecting their local culture) thought about deceased family members, particularly children. Luckily I discovered this when the sermon could be followed up, exploring our much greater Easter hope than sitting on clouds with harps, without the confusion of whether one particular child had become a guardian angel to bereaved loved ones.

There are particular pastoral minefields. Mothering Sunday is probably the greatest because we preach in the context of enormous emotional undercurrents for the childless, the bereaved, women who have had an abortion perhaps years in the past, and people whose relationship with their mother or their children was or is anything but loving. A man said to me some time after the death of his mother, 'It sounds stupid but I suddenly realized I'm an orphan.' There is a path to be trodden between the expectations of those who want to give thanks for mothers and those for whom this is a deeply ambivalent day.[16] Family services can be another trouble spot, as can any illustrations that equate family life with nuclear families. Too many family services are children's services with a children's sermon that does not nurture anyone, so aim to give children one thing to take away, not everything. Even better, give them valid responsibilities within the service so that they learn by doing rather than by hearing. A well told Bible story will engage people of all ages, and often the biblical text is all that is needed because the original authors were consummate storytellers. Our choristers love the strong narratives when they occur at Evensong; the repetition of the musical instruments when Daniel and his friends are being commanded to fall down and worship the golden image (Daniel 3) always brings a laugh, while the story of David and Goliath (1 Samuel 17) is never too familiar to lose its power, and the stories from the Apocrypha of the elephant falling on the enemy (1 Maccabees 6) and Judith's deception of Holofernes (Judith 12–13) are also favourites. The latter, like the story of Esther's exposure of Haman (Esther 7), is a masterpiece of pacing the plot, which we cannot better in our own words. Most adults have never heard the story of Ruth read in its entirety and are unaware of the story of Susanna in the Apocrypha. When I read both aloud to a group of women on a retreat there was no need for any comment from me: they engaged with the stories and a lively discussion ensued about vulnerable women in society and women unable to defend themselves against false accusation. The Godly Play approach that asks 'wondering' questions is another preaching resource for narratives.

Pastoral preaching has to be comfortable with God's silence.[17] Naming this as mystery is not a cop-out but an invitation to inhabit that silence. Church is the place to bring our experience of the silence of God and the questions it raises so that, in God's time, it is recast not as a silence of total absence but as a silence where God will meet us. Preaching can offer the encouragement to own those silences.

Prophetic preaching

When we hear the word 'prophetic' the image that usually comes to mind is that of an Old Testament prophet, raging against the waywardness of the people. The prophetic message may indeed come as a challenge, but it may come as invitation: when the disciples responded to the invitation of the risen Jesus, 'Come and have breakfast' (John 21.12), they had no idea what would ensue. Prophetic preaching is not about foretelling the future but about interpreting what is present in order that we can live more faithfully; frequently it has a strong social perspective that can be a challenge in itself.[18] But if we preach pastorally people will be more open to hear us preach prophetically. We can learn about this blend of pastoral and prophetic from a novelist's insight: the derivation of the word 'preacher' lies in 'prédicateur', an old French word meaning prophet, 'And what is the purpose of a prophet except to find meaning in trouble?'[19] – a very pastoral, prophetic vocation.

A point of entry for sermons about social issues may be God's acts in biblical and more recent history, or the wisdom literature's portrayal of what makes for a good life that we can hold before the people, tantalizing them into action. Wesley Avram suggests that exhortation to action, which often comes at the end of a sermon or speech, rests on an appeal to the audience's desire to participate in the shared ethos represented by the speaker, so preaching for ethical action rests largely on inspiring people with a common vision with which they want to be associated.[20] Rhetorical skills can aid this, since the proof and peroration in rhetoric aim to outline the desired action and encourage people to respond. Whatever our starting-point, the story of Jesus on the Emmaus road (Luke 24) provides a classic paradigm for preaching for change. Jesus comes alongside the grieving disciples and, with a few carefully chosen questions, gets them to tell their story. He then sets that story of despair alongside Scripture and reinterprets it before making himself known. Transformation results. Our approach to preaching can be the same: hear the story of the people (exegesis of the congregation), set that alongside appropriate Scripture (exegesis of the text), interpret both in the light of each other (preaching) and allow the transformation to happen.

Without the pastoral element we cannot connect with our hearers, but without the prophetic element we deny them the opportunity of transformation. So, gently but persistently, we help them to explore the underlying assumptions of their lives and expose those that are inadequate. Prophetic preaching need not be loud and angry – there may be a strong strain of sadness in it. Our preaching journey over the months and years involves walking alongside people, but also, through our prayer and study, equipping ourselves to give direction and a sense of security when we invite people to accompany us on a journey towards new ways of living. On that journey we encourage them to keep moving but also to enjoy the scenery, wonder at a spectacular vista and gaze at the horizon; we help them up the steeper or rockier paths and pause for refreshment or find temporary shelter when there is a storm. Patience is needed with the slow, guidance for those who like to run ahead, retrieval and retracing of steps for those who take a wrong turn, and a helping hand for those who find walking difficult.

Occasionally we have to preach a sermon that people don't want to hear. Unless we have won the trust of our hearers at other times they will resist us and what we have to say. It is difficult for visiting preachers to challenge congregations since there is always the excuse that 'the preacher didn't understand us'. Visiting preachers who might be able to do this successfully are people of known local or national stature, although even then there can be resistance. The Bishop of Durham referred to asylum seekers when preaching at the Cathedral at one Midnight Eucharist and was rebuked afterwards by someone in the congregation for straying from the Christmas theme. But, as the Bishop pointed out, Matthew tells us that Jesus and his family were refugees in Egypt. The temptation is to divorce the pastoral and the prophetic when the world sorely needs the prophetic element of the Christmas story.

Civic preaching

Preaching at civic services is a subset of prophetic preaching. The congregation is drawn together to mark some aspect of civic life, and the preacher's responsibility is to bring together the word of God as heard in the Bible readings and the life of the local or national community.[21] At Durham Cathedral two such services are juxtaposed in one July weekend: the Miners' Gala Festival Service on Saturday celebrates the mining heritage of County Durham and is attended by crowds of people from the former pit villages around the city, with their brass bands, banners and deep recollections of a past heritage that is fiercely remembered, followed on Sunday by Matins for the Courts of Justice, which is attended by a cross-section of people involved in the legal and judicial processes in the region.

On these occasions many people present are unfamiliar both with church worship and with listening to sermons, seeing their attendance as nothing more than a duty. It is more important than ever for the preacher to gain and hold their attention at the start, to preach in an accessible style and to give a message with substance. Sadly, instead of being seen as an opportunity for energetic and engaging Christian apology, too many civic sermons are little more than general platitudes. Now is the opportunity to proclaim Christian hope with enthusiasm and vigour, to send people away with something more than they expected, perhaps inspired to consider the relevance of Christianity to life today. Preaching at Evensong to mark the abolition of Durham City Council when emotions were palpable, the Dean set this death in the community's life in the context of the deaths faced and survived by the Cathedral in past centuries and gave new hope for the future not just in the new civic structures but in the development of tradition.[22]

On these occasions the Scriptures may be specially chosen rather than derived from the lectionary. When preaching at Matins for the Courts of Justice, I was asked by the High Sheriff to preach on the theme of 'forgiveness'[23] since that is a recurring question in the world of crime, justice and punishment. All the people in the congregation dealt on a daily basis with the stories of people's lives that have been affected one way or another by crime, and so I decided to approach this through the lens of stories in the Bible where these issues were uppermost, rather than from the legal codes in the Bible or the wisdom literature's consideration of the subject, which would have led to more philosophical sermons. The stories freed me to make links between the biblical world and the world of the Courts, and one particular aspect provoked discussion afterwards with a police chief. The congregation at this service had a common connection but no great sense of overall community – most were present as representatives. In contrast, the people attending the Miners' Gala service come in their communities and have a deep shared history and culture so that there is a strong feeling of a gathered community. A colleague, preach-

ing this service,[24] began by standing alongside the congregation
– describing the view from his childhood bedroom window in
a mining community – thus placing himself, a stranger to them,
firmly within their community in a way the rest of the clergy
could not have done. He built on that by naming parts of their
mining history in the context of Cathedral worship, honouring
it and articulating that he had not only done his homework
in exegeting the congregation but was willing to bring their
troubled history of pit closures and disasters into this place
of worship: in other words to assure them that their stories
belonged here. This gave them confidence in him to follow him
when, later in the sermon, he led them more overtly into the
Christian tradition and made connections for them.

National or local tragedies

When tragedy strikes, whether nationally or locally, more
people go to church but the tragedy, not God, is uppermost in
most people's minds and they expect the preacher to address the
subject one way or another.[25] That does not mean that we hand
the whole sermon over to it, making the tragedy rather than
God the focus. The liturgy can do some of the work and provide a stability and direction for the congregation – I remember
a service the day after a local tragedy when the Easter hymns
and Easter hope did not deny the sorrow but nurtured a deep
resurrection joy and comfort.

Most preachers were not expecting to be functioning primarily as pastors when they anticipated their sermons on the
Fourteenth Sunday after Trinity in 2001. Yet there cannot have
been a single sermon preached that day that did not address the
seeming chasm that had opened up between belief and experience five days earlier on September 11. The lectionary Old
Testament reading was either Jeremiah 4, which includes the
line 'the whole land shall be a desolation', or Exodus 31, where
Moses pleads with God to stay his anger against the wayward
people; Psalm 14 has the assertion by a fool that there is no

God; 1 Timothy 1 speaks of God's redemption of Paul from his former violence against the Church; and the parables of the lost sheep and the lost coin in Luke 15 speak of God's relentless search for the lost. These were rich resources for interpreting world events, and the greatest pastoral service we can give may be to hold traumatic experience in the light of the whole of the biblical record and the tradition of the faith, rather than pick off one specially chosen, comforting, section of it.

I was preaching that Sunday at a village church I did not know. I arrived to distressed confusion over the use of the fairly new *Common Worship*. It was clear that the correct pastoral decision was to change to 1662, which many were mistakenly expecting, because its familiarity was helpful when so much else was in turmoil and it freed the people to listen attentively to Scripture and the sermon. This familiar liturgy enabled the trauma to be placed in the context of worship in this old church, where for centuries people had brought to God, in faith, their hopes and fears, their exaltation and anguish, thus beginning to defuse the trauma and relax its grip. A specially planned service would have had to work much harder to achieve this.

I began my sermon by articulating the confusion and setting it in a wider context so that from the start it was clear that we were not in totally unexplored territory as far as the Christian faith was concerned.

'When the firestorm came more than 40,000 people died there. I think this was the first time I cried out for God. My question was not "Why could God allow this to happen?" but "Where is God?" I am still looking for the answer to that question.'

That may sound like the disbelief and despair of an atheist, but it is not. They are the words of Jürgen Moltmann whose family all died in Hamburg, who was conscripted by Hitler and captured by the British and Canadians who imprisoned him in a POW camp in Kilmarnock. There he was given a New Testament and Psalms by the chaplain and began to piece together the shreds of his despair and disillusionment with the lies and evil of Nazism into faith. He went on to become one of the twentieth century's greatest theologians who is known for his exploration of suffering, and of the hope of God's reign. His question 'Where is God?' has sustained and driven his theological studies, but from a position of faith.

In the light of events this week, where is God? We may go on asking that question all our lives and it is good that we do so. If we only ask, 'How can someone do this terrible thing?' we will end up in despair as we are confronted with the depth of human evil. But if we ask 'Where is God?' we embark on a pilgrimage towards God.

There were five days in which to prepare that sermon but sometimes events give much less time: the death of the Princess of Wales on a Saturday evening was probably the most demanding example, and the skill in such situations is not to write a new sermon from scratch but to integrate the changed circumstances with the anticipated sermon. Thus, already preaching to an unfamiliar congregation in the dual context of his own installation and beginning of his new ministry and the Cathedral's St Cuthbert's Day celebrations, the Dean of Durham had to make last-minute changes because the invasion of Iraq earlier that day introduced a third and very divergent focus for people's attention.

Preaching at the pastoral offices

At the occasional offices people who have not been in church for a long time attend and may be on edge about being there. It is unlikely that they know each other so there is no sense of worshipping with one another; instead they are there as individuals to see something happen. Everything may be strange: the order of service, posture, singing, listening to Bible readings. Wedding guests may regard the sermon as an intrusion that is delaying the party, whereas at a funeral people often see it as the most important part of the service and hope the preacher will help them begin to sort out their grief. It is in these very mixed and unarticulated contexts that we are charged with pastoral preaching, and we may find ourselves doing so against a backdrop of babies crying, people weeping and others fidgeting. No one at pastoral offices takes in everything that is said, however hard they try, so it is a good idea to give the principal people (including godparents at a baptism) a clean copy of the sermon to read again later on. This can be handed to the best man at a wedding or one of the family at a baptism or funeral.

Funerals and other services in times of sadness or confusion

The liturgy is the work of the people, and funerals are hard work for those who attend. Our focus for the sermon is given and our pastoral task – the function of the sermon – is to begin to build a bridge for the mourners to walk on between their experience and the good news of the gospel. They may not tread it immediately but they need to know where to find it. By setting the funeral in the context of a journey upon which the mourners have been thrust, we are holding out hope and the possibility of a future without the deceased. We do not try to convert the mourners but offer them the faith of the Christian Church, inviting them to turn to Christ in the days and weeks to come. We need to work with the liturgy, which refuses mourners the false luxury of denial that death has occurred but opens the door for new life to come out of death: theologically the cross is at the heart of Christianity. Naming the death is a hard but essential comfort, and the liturgy does it more eloquently than we can manage; our opportunity is to set that particular life and death in the light of the gospel.

Exegeting the congregation will tell us that, in addition to the bereaved family, other people will recall their own past bereavements. There may be disenfranchised grievers at the back – the mistress, the divorced spouse, the estranged sibling

– whose past relationship to the deceased person cannot be acknowledged publicly. Family dynamics may be so bad that the preacher has to be the person who briefly but publicly names the disarray so that it ceases to exert its control over the service, before then bringing the gospel's light to the tangled mess.[26] If we are ourselves reeling, angry or confused we must find adequate support for ourselves. For this reason, it is not always a good idea to preach at the funeral of a close family member; we may need to be free to be a mourner.

Preaching at funerals is always at short notice. We don't have to do all the pastoral work in one sermon but should be alongside people at this crucial moment, pointing them to God and holding out the hope of the gospel rather than having answers for which they ask but are not ready. Instead they want to know that God is there and to be given permission to ask questions and to grieve. As Peter Hawkins points out, while we cannot offer information about the world to come, we can hold out hope and we can encourage people to open up their ability to hope and to face the unknown with courage rather than fear. He suggests that the best way to preach the world to come is to court it respectfully from a distance, recognizing our profound ignorance but yet our faith that everything is 'so much, much, much more' and we have only hints and guesses, intuitions and dreams. Using our imagination, we can stand at the threshold and imagine taking a first step into the city of God.[27]

Concentration spans are short, so it is not a time for abstract phrases or concepts nor for illustrations beyond those arising from the person's life or the Scripture reading. Simple and familiar words and phrases help, and the use of the person's name is important – we are not burying anybody but somebody. David Schlafer advocates honouring the life of the deceased not by telling the whole story as in a eulogy but by carefully identifying one aspect of it – a vivid image, a rich metaphor or an illuminating anecdote – to capture a sense of the life and of the transition which the funeral represents.[28] In other words, preach inductively from the specific to the general and use the faceting approach to take one facet of the life and examine it in the light of Scripture, so that people are given a fresh perspective on the person's life and death and pointed to the resurrection power of God in the face of their grieving.

It is not the time for a full theology of death and resurrection although our pastoral responsibility requires us to be theological in our preaching. The seasons of the church year can be a helpful resource when preaching at a funeral. One of my first funerals was three days before Christmas so, rather than ignore the Christmas preparations all around us, the natural approach was to acknowledge the tension that the world was preparing to celebrate Christmas while we gathered to mourn a loved man, to acknowledge – as I did early in my homily – that in the midst of the season of birth we were in the season of death. The homily concluded with suggestions for how the family could use the Christmas season to help them in their grieving.

One of the names of Jesus, which we remember particularly at Christmas, is 'Emmanuel'; translated it means quite simply, 'God with us'. God is with us in life and in death, because we are the Lord's possession. We believe that God has come among us: born as a child in Bethlehem, God has entered our history and made it his own – thus making us his own. And Bill[29] knew that. He believed in God's love for him, and lived his life on the premise that the message of Christmas is true – God is with us.

So, for Bill, we can rejoice that God has given him the Christmas gift of being in the Lord's presence. In the gospel reading we heard Jesus' promise to the people he loved that, having prepared a place for them in heaven, he would come again, and take them to himself so that where he is, they would be also. That is what Jesus did for Bill last Friday, he came to him and took him to himself – God is with us, Emmanuel. That is the ultimate Christmas gift – the gift of dying in the Lord and thus being in God's presence eternally.

If we can rejoice for Bill, we can also grieve for him. Grief is an expression of love that has been lost, and the ability to grieve is itself a gift of God. But we do not grieve as those without hope. This Christmas may be especially hard because the world around is celebrating and seems to have no place for death and grief. But I encourage you, as you sing the words of Christmas carols this year and hear the story of Jesus' birth, to remember that whether we live or die we are the Lord's possession; and to hold on to the truth that Bill knew, that millions through the ages have known, that in life and death Emmanuel, God is with us.

The same seasonal resources are available to us at other times of the year opening up different possible frameworks in which to place and hold the particular bereavement. From Advent's tenacious hope to Lent's portrayal of Jesus being tested almost to breaking-point, Easter's message of resurrection from the dead and Ascension's assurance that we are raised in Christ, to Pentecost's empowering to go on without the day-by-dayness of Jesus' physical presence, there are rich homiletic pickings to be had.[30] The hymns chosen may give a springboard for a homily that the family might continue to associate with that hymn in the future, as may phrases from the liturgy.

In my experience, if people feel comfortable and are treated gently at a funeral, and if they hear good news that meets them in their present situation, they may come back to the church that has made them welcome. I can think of many people who eventually came back to church primarily because of the bridge that was built at a funeral.

Baptisms and marriages

Baptisms and marriages are essentially joyful pastoral services, and part of our pastoral ministry is to articulate that joy and thankfulness in the context of worship. When preaching at a baptism keep in mind that, for the Church, the word of God and the sacrament of baptism are important, for the family there is their own family life and story, while framing all of this is the Easter context of all baptisms, whatever time of year, and the message of dying and rising to new life in Christ. To hold these disparate foci together, preaching through the symbols of water, light and oil can be helpful.

When preaching at a marriage, the best option is to preach to both couple and congregation, since it honours the presence of everyone at the marriage, inviting everyone to take their part in establishing this marriage. On one occasion I was preaching at a marriage in the Cathedral on the anniversary of the Cathedral's founding and began the sermon,

> Today is the anniversary of the foundation of this Cathedral in 1093, so it is the Cathedral's 914th birthday. That seems a very appropriate day to celebrate a wedding because we are in a part of the Cathedral which, over those 914 years, has heard hundreds of people make vows. Some have been couples, like Andrew and Alison,[31] but far more were monks because for 450 years this Quire was where the monks worshipped and where new monks made their vows while the community gathered round them prayed for them. Since this was a Benedictine monastery, the vows that have been made here, time and again, are those of stability, obedience and conversion of life. And I want to suggest that, although Andrew and Alison have no intention of being monks, those three vows are at the heart of what they are promising to each other in the sight of God and with our prayers.

I then explored, briefly, the meaning and relevance of stability, obedience and conversion of life in our own lives today, including, but not only, within marriage. One of the guests said afterward it was the most helpful marriage sermon she had heard because it was realistic about the demands of marriage but the mention of other vows gave her something to think about for herself.

If we are preaching pastorally at joyful services we need to keep in mind, but not be controlled by, pastoral needs among the congregation for whom this particular service exacerbates sorrow, which (unlike at funerals) it is not acceptable to express. At the baptism of a baby, childless people or parents who have lost their children for any one of several reasons can find their pain resurfacing. Marriages are attended by single people, parents who don't approve of their child's choice of partner, married people whose relationships have failed or are failing and people who remember growing up in unhappy families. In these situations the pastoral approach to preaching is to preach inductively, to keep the focus on this particular marriage and uphold the ideal of Christian marriage without conveying messages about other people's situations. Since we proclaim God's grace and invitation to transformed living, there are wider ramifications for all and the sermon can hold out the possibility of new beginnings in any and all of our relationships with one another.

Preaching on ethical issues

Ethical issues can rarely be addressed adequately in passing, but need a sermon or study session to themselves with opportunity for discussion and questions. Otherwise our hearers may be dissatisfied with what is said, or abandon the thread of the sermon having been distracted by the ethical question when it was mentioned. When preaching on an ethical issue it needs to be the focus of the sermon – that does not mean that it cannot be approached through Scripture, including the lectionary Scriptures for the day, but the focus of engagement with the Scriptures should be the ethical question, which should be identified and explained. It can then be considered in the light of the Christian tradition, noting that many contemporary ethical issues raise questions that the Bible does not address directly although it is full of narratives that put flesh on the bones of ethical issues – the dilemma faced by Saul's armour-bearer when asked to kill his badly injured master (1 Samuel 31 and 2 Samuel 1) doesn't give guidelines for euthanasia but does illustrate the way that he and David differed over the request in an age where there could be no medical intervention. We have to be very careful how we handle Scripture to ensure integrity, not making it say something it never intended.

We have a responsibility to provide reliable information about ethical issues but do not have to preach a didactic sermon. Other relevant information from the secular world – in the case of euthanasia, for example, medical evidence about death, dying and palliative care – is relevant, and we have a duty to our hearers to do our research well and to represent the findings accurately. When it is time to draw conclusions or guidelines, these should be clear for people who have not thought this through until this moment, and should where possible apply the insights of the sermon to contemporary life. It is important to remember that some in the congregation will be hearing this sermon not just as an abstract discussion of an ethical issue but as a deeply personal sermon – they may be struggling with thoughts that they wish an elderly and suffering relative would die, or handling a sense of guilt as they wonder if they did everything possible for someone who has died. Therefore there should always be a pastoral component to our preaching on ethical matters and an implicit invitation to those for whom this is more than an academic exercise to come to talk things through privately.[32]

In all our preaching, even on one of the routine Sundays after Pentecost when nothing much has happened to demand our attention and most people are on holiday, someone will need to hear the pastoral and the prophetic elements in our preaching. We proclaim a God who, even before the incarnation, shared our suffering and who is always bringing new life out of death: 'I have observed the misery of my people and have heard their cry . . . I have come down to deliver them' (Exodus 3.7, 8). It is our responsibility to speak this hope into the situations of the faithful people who come to church week by week.

Notes

1 Paul Bull, *Lectures on Preaching and Sermon Construction*, SPCK, London, 1922, pp. 116, 119.

2 James Fowler has helpfully identified six stages of faith through which people may pass during their lifetime from Stage 1 in childhood to Stage 6, which many do not reach. The adult stages (3–6) mark a progression from conventional faith, when a person is sure of their beliefs, shares the faith of the majority and has a strong sense of rules and religious authority, through more individualized faith, to ability to live with paradox and finally a sense of feeling at one with God and being willing to give oneself to a larger cause without regard to personal cost. Familiarity with the stages of faith is helpful for preachers. See James Fowler, *Stages of Faith*, Harper & Row, San Francisco, 1981.

3 Augustine, *First Catechetical Instruction*, trans. Joseph P. Christopher, Ancient Christian Writers, 2, Newman Press, Westminster, MD, 1946, p. 50.

4 See, for example, Helen Cameron, Douglas Davies, Philip Richter and Frances Ward (eds), *Studying Local Churches: A Handbook*, SCM Press, London, 2005.

5 Mary Alice Mulligan, 'Teaching Disciples to Preach in the Service of Word and Table', in Michael Monshau (ed.), *Preaching at the Double Feast: Homiletics for Eucharistic Worship*, Liturgical Press, Collegeville, MN, 2006, p. 60.

6 Laura Tubbs Tisdale, *Preaching as Local Theology and Folk Art*, Augsburg Fortress, Minneapolis, 1997, p. 46.

7 Thomas G. Long, *The Witness of Preaching*, Westminster John Knox, Louisville, 1989, pp. 78–9.

8 Professor Peter Hawkins, *The Preacher's Divine Comedy*, Lyman Beecher Lectures at Yale Divinity School October 2007, Yale Divinity School, www.yale.edu/divinity/vidoe/convo2007/beecher03.shtml, accessed 9 January 2009.

9 Tubbs Tisdale, *Preaching as Local Theology and Folk Art*, p. 53.

10 Walter Brueggemann, 'The Preacher, Text and People', *Theology Today* 47 (October 1990), pp. 237–47.

11 For example, in the Church of England, Ordained Local Ministers, some Non Stipendiary Ministers or Ministers in Secular Employment and Readers, and their equivalents in other Churches, who serve in the church which originally helped them identify their vocation.

12 The Diocese of Oxford has excellent and practical guidance on its website about how to welcome people with autism and Asperger syndrome in church: http://oxford.anglican.org/documents/6876.pdf.

13 See Sally A. Brown, 'When Lament Shapes the Sermon', in Sally A. Brown and Patrick D. Miller (eds), *Lament: Reclaiming Practices*

in Pulpit, Pew and Public Square, Westminster John Knox, Louisville, 2005. See also Durham Cathedral Sermons: 9 March 2008, 'Lamentations', Canon Rosalind Brown.

14 Durham Cathedral Sermons: 12 November 2006, 'On Remembrance Sunday', The Very Revd Michael Sadgrove; 27 January 2008, 'Holocaust and Obedience', Canon Ian Jagger; 27 January 2008, 'Holocaust Memorial Day', The Very Revd Michael Sadgrove; 21 September 2008, 'Investment and Liberation', Canon Stephen Cherry.

15 For examples, see Durham Cathedral Sermons: 8 October 2006, 'Cantus firmus: The Enduring Melody', Canon Rosalind Brown; 17 June 2007, 'Letting Go in Love', Canon Rosalind Brown; 13 January 2008, 'Jesus' Baptism and Our Baptism', Canon David Kennedy; 20 January 2008, 'Our Baptismal Calling', Canon Rosalind Brown; 11 November 2007, 'Light Up a Life', The Very Revd Michael Sadgrove; 8 October 2006, 'Jesus on Marriage', Canon David Brown; 22 January 2006, 'Wedding Banquets', Canon Rosalind Brown.

16 For examples of sermons on Mothering Sunday, see Durham Cathedral Sermons: 2 March 2008, 'Sons and Parents', Canon Rosalind Brown; 18 March 2007, 'The Feminine in the Parable of the Prodigal Son', Canon David Brown.

17 Durham Cathedral Sermons: 22 February 2009, 'Still Small Voice', The Very Revd Michael Sadgrove.

18 Durham Cathedral Sermons: 20 August 2006, 'Stewardship of God's Land', Canon Rosalind Brown; 21 September 2008, 'Investment and Poverty', Canon Stephen Cherry; 5 October 2008, 'Gotcha!', Canon Stephen Cherry; 17 May 2009, 'Three Degrees', The Very Revd Michael Sadgrove.

19 Marilynne Robinson, *Gilead*, Virago, London, 2005, pp. 266–7.

20 Wesley D. Avram, 'Exhortation', in Thomas O. Sloane (ed.), *Encyclopaedia of Rhetoric*, Oxford University Press, Oxford, 2001, pp. 279ff.

21 Durham Cathedral Sermons: 9 September 2007, 'For the Durham University Alumni', The Very Revd Michael Sadgrove; 17 February 2008, 'A Sermon to Honour the Rifles', The Very Revd Michael Sadgrove.

22 Durham Cathedral Sermons: 11 March 2009, 'Farewell to Durham City Council', The Very Revd Michael Sadgrove.

23 Durham Cathedral Sermons: 9 July 2006, 'Forgiveness', Canon Rosalind Brown.

24 Durham Cathedral Sermons: 14 July 2007, 'Miners Festival', Canon David Kennedy.

25 The same principle applies to services on days that have particular associations – even if a service on Mothering Sunday is not focused on that, some acknowledgement of the day is needed for pastoral

reasons. A service I attended one Remembrance Day made no attempt to acknowledge the day in any way beyond interrupting the service to keep two minutes' silence a few minutes before 11 o'clock and thus missed a pastoral and prophetic responsibility.

26 Durham Cathedral Sermons: 5 November 2006, 'Speak No Evil of the Dead', Canon David Brown.

27 Peter Hawkins, *The Preacher's Divine Comedy*.

28 David J. Schlafer, *What Makes This Day Different?*, Cowley Publications, Cambridge, MA, 1998, pp. 35–45.

29 The name has been changed.

30 For further insights, see Barbara Schmitz, *The Life of Christ and the Death of a Loved One: Crafting the Funeral Homily*, CSS, Lima, OH, 1995 and Schlafer, *What Makes This Day Different?*

31 The names have been changed.

32 See David Schlafer and Timothy Sedgwick, *Preaching What we Practice: Proclamation and Moral Discernment*, Morehouse Publishing, Harrisburg, PA, 2007.

8

PREPARING TO PREACH

Wondering with the Scriptures

By now it should be clear that I believe the most important preparation for preaching does not occur in the pulpit or even the study. We cannot hope to preach effectively if we do not live effectively; simply mastering the techniques of sermon preparation will not equip us to be faithful preachers. But there comes a time when we have to prepare a specific sermon and we want it to be the best it can be, attaining John Killinger's ideal, 'There is something artful about a well-made sermon. The ideas march, the phrases do their work, the illustrations release their light at the proper moments, the climax is achieved and the point made with all the finesse at the command of the preacher.'[1] All that is easier said than done, and what follows is but one condensed perspective on the subject, which uses Psalm 137 as an illustration; wider reading from experienced preachers in a variety of traditions will help to fill this out and suggest other approaches. We are all different and our own way of preparation to preach develops with experience, so experimentation will help us discover what works best for us and for the people who hear us. It is a bit like learning to drive, when even turning left takes immense concentration but eventually becomes instinctive.

Normally we know in advance that we will be preaching and we do ourselves and our hearers a disservice if we do not begin preparation early.[2] We are all prone to over-work and to exhaustion so it makes sense to begin in good time and, since we have to give time to sermon preparation sooner or later (a rule of thumb for beginners is an hour of preparation to a minute of sermon, although that should reduce with experience), to maximize the use of that time by beginning early. This gives enough time for us to get over our first ideas and put them out of the way – like a sweet pea where the first shoot needs to be pinched out, the later growth is often stronger. While none of us is immune to occasional last-minute preparation, no one should experience regular panicked fighting of tiredness while writing a sermon on Saturday night when we should be watching TV with the family. Philips Brooks was uncompromising about Saturday night sermon-writing: 'That . . . I count as the crowning disgrace of a man's ministry. It is dishonest. It is giving but the last flicker of the week as it sinks in its socket, to those who, simply to talk about it as a bargain, have paid for the full light burning at its brightest.'[3] It is a lame excuse that by leaving it all to the last minute we can preach to the real-life situation of the congregation; if we know our congregation we'll have a good idea what makes their worlds tick. If God does inspire a new thought on the morning the sermon is to be preached it can be incorporated into the already prepared sermon.

Three weeks in advance – preparatory work

This might sound frightening: beginning a sermon this far in advance! However, our initial work can begin while other sermons are still in preparation and consists in familiarizing ourselves with the Scriptures, simply living with them, prayerfully reading them (in the order in which people will hear them on Sunday) in different translations, reading them slowly, paying attention to the words not just the sentences. Reading them aloud helps (Nietzsche said the German people do not read with their ears 'but only with their eyes; to read they put their ears in the drawer'[4]), and it never ceases to amaze me how something completely new strikes me because I have heard someone else read the words. This initial engagement is best done away from our study because of its associations with sermon writing;[5] I do it in the morning as part of my daily Bible reading. Our attitude is wondering vulnerability to the text, letting it read us, allowing it to silence us so that we have the humility to let it open the conversation with us. The congregation needs our engagement rather than our contact with Scripture. We can become so familiar with the Bible that it ceases to surprise us and, if we know the passage or have preached on it before, a past insight or sermon may come to mind as we read the passage afresh for the first time, like the punchline of a familiar joke. In that case, it helps to acknowledge that prior meeting, particularly any strong associations or ideas that have been formative for us, then put them to one side so that we are ready for fresh encounter and formation. The advantage of being immersed in the readings for two or three sermons at one time is that we get a sense of continuity, ideas from one week may carry forward into the next, or two sermons can be planned to complement each other.

Ten days in advance – beginning to explore the text

Sometimes it helps to print the words out [6] and adjust the layout or start adding annotations when themes and possibilities for further exploration come to mind. Highlighting or drawing lines between words and themes that recur helps to identify patterns. In the case of Psalm 137, laying it out in four sections (rather than the NRSV's three) allows the separation of verse 4, which seems to be a crucial question at the heart of the psalmist's musing. Verses 1–3 lead up to the question, setting the context out of which it comes. Verses 5–6 attempt to move to an answer, and also affirm hope that one day there will again be a song of Zion sung in Zion. Verses 7–9 articulate the shadow side of the hope of verses 5–6 and vent fury at the whole situation. The three larger sections are about different things – Babylon (exile), memories of Jerusalem (home) and Babylon and Edom (enemies). They are also about the present, the past and the future; about paralysis, intentional action, desired action; about the actions of others, their own actions, desired actions by God and others.

In the layout below, the bold text identifies places and the indentation the things that happened there. Bold italics highlight the theme of remembering and forgetting; speech and sound words are italicized and uppercase words are associated with emotion.

1   By the **rivers of Babylon** –
     there we sat down and **there** we WEPT
     when we *remembered* **Zion**.

2   On the **willows there**
     we *hung up our harps*.

3   For **there** our captors
     asked us for *songs*,
     and our tormentors *asked* for MIRTH, *saying*
     '*Sing* us one of the *songs* of **Zion**!'

4   How could we *sing* the LORD's *song*
     in a **foreign land**?

5   If I *forget* you, O **Jerusalem**,
     let my right hand wither!

6   Let my *tongue* cling to the roof of my mouth,
     if I do not *remember* you,
     if I do not set **Jerusalem**
     above my highest JOY.

7   *Remember*, O LORD, against the **Edomites**
     the day of **Jerusalem's** fall,
     how they *said*, 'Tear it down! Tear it down!
     Down to its foundations!'

8   O daughter **Babylon**, you devastator!
     HAPPY shall they be who pay you back
     what you have done to us!

9   HAPPY shall they be who take your little ones
      and dash them against the rock!

From this visual laying-out of the text, several themes for
exploration immediately suggest themselves in this time when
curiosity and imagination take the lead. Geography is clearly
important, with several places being named; speech words
communicate strong emotion: 'wept', 'sing', 'mirth', 'tongue
cleave to the roof of my mouth', 'they said "Tear it down, Tear
it down"'. The psalm begins with Israel weeping in Babylon,
a foreign land, and ends with a desire that Babylon be forced
to weep in a foreign land (a rocky environment, in contrast to
Babylon's flat riverbanks); remembering or forgetting begins
each of the NRSV's strophes, and each ends with a pleasant
emotion (mirth, joy, happiness), although the first and last are
ironic.

We are not preparing a sermon but living with the Scriptures
and letting them work on us. So ask the reading questions and
let it address us, challenge us or surprise us. What stands out
or niggles? Where is the conflict or the trouble? Does it connect
with the other readings set for the day, heard in previous weeks
or coming soon after? Where is the good news? Working with
Psalm 137, feel the memory and disappointment, anger and
pleading with God; sit down and be an exile, weeping even
though we do not know all the details of their exile, why the
Edomites and Babylonians are so loathsome to the psalmist, or
the significance of the geographical places mentioned. There
will be time to explore them later. Play with different perspectives and enter the scene: in Mark 5 be Jairus' wife, one of the
disciples, one of the professional mourners, the little girl; in
John 20 be Mary, Peter, John, the angel, Jesus (was he watching
all this going on?). In Corinthians hear Paul's uncompromising letter being read to us in a gathering of that cosmopolitan
church. Try the traditional spiritual approach of 'composition
of place': imagine what is going on. Who is there? What are
they wearing? Are they sitting or standing? What colours do
we see? What sounds do we hear? Are there any smells? How

long does the action take? What tone of voice is used? What is the weather like? What emotions do we feel?

Take time to mull the text over and incubate it when walking or standing in a queue; perhaps learn the passage and see what insights are sparked by speaking rather than reading it. Try emphasizing different words and use some ideas in the chapter on imagination; if words don't come easily, play appropriate music, or use whatever art form helps us walk in the world of the biblical reading. At the time I was preparing this sermon, a newspaper picture of an old man sitting on a pile of rubble in Gaza joined an old picture of a child being driven away in a cattle truck from the ruins of Bosnia in my visual resources, while my wonderings on paper included,

Riverbanks
Flat, expansive, irrigated
Cruelly, relentlessly
Alienate
Exiles

Jerusalem
Mountainous, familiar, desecrated
Distantly, relentlessly
Calls
Home

Babylonians
Captors, taskmasters, pagans
Tauntingly, vindictively
Demand
Mirth

Exiles
Powerless, betrayed, isolated
Boldly, faithfully
Refuse
Compliance

Musicians
Captive, tormented, weeping
Desperately, hopelessly
Become
Mutes

Revenge
Pent-up, seething, murderous
Graphically, desperately
Seeks
Justice.

This is our time with God centred on the reading, and the energy in the eventual sermon may well lie with the energy in our early wondering encounter with the text.

A week before preaching: begin to work more closely with the Scriptures

A practical question to consider is the environment in which we work: is it conducive to concentration and creativity? Different people work best in different physical spaces, and Alan Bennett goes so far as to say that what he is wearing affects his ability to write (he can't write in shorts or with no shirt because writing is a kind of divestment so that if he starts off undressed he has nowhere to go).[7] For many people, writing space is a compromise between the possible and preferable but attention to this question of our environment may be helpful. Equally some people work best writing longhand, others with a computer.

Select the primary Scripture for the sermon

It is now time to start to narrow your focus. As we pray for the people to whom we will preach, which Scriptures (don't forget the psalm) are emerging as the one or ones from which to preach? Are there links between readings that can be explored helpfully or is the juxtaposition best ignored for preaching purposes?

Study the Scriptures

Having chosen the text(s) that will form the basis of the sermon, work with them in more depth. Use one translation (not a paraphrase) as the principal text, but refer to others. Read around the text, going back into the previous chapters and forward to the next to get a sense of this particular reading in context. If the passage is related to others look at them too: the prophets and the history books often address the same period in the nation's life from different perspectives, while Acts, Revelation and the epistles can shed different light on the same church. Look for the natural beginning and ending of the passage and for any divisions within it. Where do the pericopes[8] start and stop? Would changing the boundaries of the reading give added clarity or set the context (the lectionary permits the extension of readings)?

Someone has said that we should worry the text like a dog worries a bone: keep going back to it from different angles. Resist the temptation to begin with commentaries; they are our servants not our masters, so note any questions and use the commentaries to help with them rather than to filter engagement with the text or to 'tell you what it means'. When commentaries are our masters, the resulting sermon will be close to an academic lecture or (worse) an academic paper. Don't automatically defer to them; we may have further insights than those they give as definitive. Having said that, our preaching should be well-grounded academically, and all preachers need good basic resources of commentaries and text books; a reliable one-volume Bible commentary[9] can be supplemented with commentaries on individual books, not necessarily all from the same series since variety broadens our insight. Other essential reference books include a dictionary of the Bible, a

PREPARING TO PREACH (1)

concordance, a Bible atlas and books that provide historical and cultural information about the life at different times in the biblical record. If we have an account of a journey, finding out how long it is and the landscape may be very telling: Elijah's journey to Zarephath was not a short hop by chariot but a walk through 100 miles of land ravaged by famine: enough to test even his faith in God's ability to provide.

As Craddock recognized, it is exciting to let Scripture lead and commentaries help us. Most of what we discover will underlie rather than be explicit in our sermon – better that the people catch our enthusiasm for biblical study and are spurred to try for themselves than that we give them every last undiluted word of exegesis and put them off study for life. The congregation will know very quickly if the exegesis has been done but they do not need to know all its fruit. They want to hear a sermon, not a study paper; to be opened to transformation not merely fed information.

Some of the questions that an initial reading of Psalm 137 raises include the historical situation that gave rise to the psalm, the identity of the 'we', what difference it makes if the psalm is stopped at verse 6, what the Edomites and Babylonians had done and the ethics of the sentiments in verse 9. Rummaging around Bible footnotes, atlases, commentaries and text books yielded the following:[10]

Historical background (2 Kings 24–25; 2 Chronicles 36; Jeremiah 37–39)

597 Jerusalem surrendered to the Babylonians. Puppet king.

589–587 Blockade of city following revolt; people slowly starved to death. Edom (Israel's relative and former ally) failed to come to the nation's help, turned against her, betrayed her to the Babylonians and encouraged them in Jerusalem's destruction (Obadiah 10–14; Ezekiel 25.12–14; 35.5–9).

587 Babylonians burned Jerusalem, razed it to the ground including the temple, executed leading citizens and

priests, deported others. Temple pillars broken and carried with the temple treasures to Babylon, probably on the backs of the humiliated captives.

In Babylon
- Exiles allowed their own settlements; some freedom to carry on life as before but material comfort was no substitute for the humiliation and loss of identity.
- Geographically, Babylon was totally unlike Judah.
  - o Jerusalem surrounded by rocky mountains, depended on wells and tunnels for water.
  - o Babylon on the flat, low-lying sand of the Euphrates river plain, subject to flooding with rivers and irrigation canals everywhere.
- Fall of Jerusalem and exile raised new and difficult questions about God, the gods of other nations, and faith.
  - o Is God now the enemy?
  - o What of Jerusalem as God's eternal earthly dwelling, or of God's promise to David of a never-ending dynasty?
  - o Exposure to Babylon's wealth and power opened their eyes to magnificence beyond anything in Jerusalem and questions whether the Babylonian gods were more than mere idols.
  - o In exile, were they punished forever by the God they had trusted? (Isaiah 63.18–19; Ezekiel 37.11). Could God save them in a foreign land? Was there to be any end to their suffering? (Psalm 74.9–11).
- Many Jews assimilated into Babylonian culture. Others remained faithful but reshaped their faith as non-temple worship emerged.
- The longing for return to their homeland never abated; prophets spoke of ultimate restoration (Jeremiah 32.6–15; Ezekiel 37).
- Former temple musicians pressed into service as court musicians and required to use their sacred songs as entertainment.

Nebuchadnezzar died:
- Babylon fell to the Persians; Cyrus' edict (538) allowed Jews to return to Jerusalem to re-establish worship and rebuild temple (Ezra 1.2–4; 6.3–5).
- Some Jews returned and began the hard task of rebuilding life in the devastated land.

Psalm 137 in this context
Too vivid for post-exilic writing so probably written in Babylon, perhaps when the Persian conquest was anticipated (accounts for vv. 8–9: hope of Babylon's punishment)?
- In the Psalter it follows two psalms celebrating the gift of the land to the people of Israel and God's defeat of the nations. The contrast through this juxtaposition is stark and inescapable.

Who are 'we'?
Given the generally humane treatment of the exiles as a whole in Babylon, the torment of v. 3 suggests a specific situation, perhaps temple musicians forced to play in the Babylonian court.
- This is more than playing Strauss waltzes at the entrance to Auschwitz, it is intentional humiliation (NB: Nazis forced Jews to burn their Talmud scrolls in public and to dance and sing, 'We rejoice that the shit is burning').[11]
- Demand that they sing to entertain a pagan public was experienced as torment: too private and personal for such exposure. Secular music, maybe; the songs of Zion, never.
- Singers announced the presence of God to the people; to refuse to sing was a devastating public declaration of the Lord's absence.

Verses 1–4: Exile in Babylon
- People have given up the unequal task of being faithful to their vocation as temple singers, now ordered to prostitute their sacred songs as entertainment in a foreign land.
- Perhaps the psalm of temple musicians at the end of their

lives, passing faith/story to the next generation – fidelity to Jerusalem not entirely dimmed?
- Temple singers had carried their harps from Jerusalem: had hoped to sing the Lord's song (NB Etty Hillesum, 'We entered the camp (Auschwitz) singing').
- But now they have hung up their harps – expression of fidelity to Jerusalem or devastating loss of hope? People set aside in Jerusalem to lead others in worship, to keep the memory of the temple songs alive, can no longer bring themselves to do it. Others will suffer – it takes the joyful remembrance of Jerusalem out of collective memory. A weighty load to bear – to be so paralysed by grief that others are denied their heritage of song. (NB when preaching to church musicians: the responsibility they bear for keeping faithful song alive).

Everything the people saw reminded them that this was not home.
- Location in verse 1: not just geographic but carries the weight of alienation, homelessness and yearning: 'We are surrounded by rivers and open, flat lands; yet our home is in the enclosed, rugged mountains.'
- A psalm from exile, exile that hurts in every way. Waters of Babylon reinforce the thirst of the soul and its refusal to be comforted, in contrast to the still waters of Psalm 23.2 where the Lord leads and restores the soul.
- Remembering Zion (v. 1) is painful, but amnesia is not an option for these exiles.
- Psalm 79 and Lamentations spell out the horror of what has happened to Zion.
- Sitting – the posture of mourning (Job 2.8, 13).
- Silence, except for weeping, is the sound of the first two verses. Rhythmic repetition of 'there we' (v. 1) echoes the rocking motion of grief.
- Is this the weeping of suffering leading to despair or the weeping that clings to belief that one's dignity as made in the image of God means one cannot but weep in the face of

a situation that is fundamentally wrong and in which God weeps too?

Various ways to read verse 4:
- A straightforward question: 'How could we sing the LORD's song in a foreign land?'
  - o The answer (v. 2): they could not.
  - o Almost an ontological impossibility because to sing the song is to remember, to bring the past into the present (cf. Passover: 'this is the night').
  - o This present is at odds with the realities of freedom and deliverance that Passover and temple worship recall.
  - o So the song could not be sung.
- But it seems more than 'could we or couldn't we?'; it is the more demanding *'in what way* could we sing the Lord's song in exile?'
  - o They do not want to forget; song can keep memory alive.
  - o They could not sing using their harps because they have hung them up.
  - o So how could they go on singing, but not in the traditional way?

This reading makes the question less a rhetorical question and more a genuine expression of distress and searching for an answer to pass on to the next generation.
- Theological issue of God's authority outside of Judah: could they sing God's song at all in exile? Was Babylon under the power of Babylonian gods?
  - o Eventually they came to a new understanding of God as the God over all nations who could be worshipped anywhere and whose purposes were not thwarted by exile.
  - o Song was related to the temple but they had no temple. Given the new situation (the emergence of synagogue worship?), how do they restore the cultic song?
  - o If they retain the hope of the restoration of the temple

– particularly if the psalm was written when Persian invasion seemed possible – how do they keep the temple songs living in memory so that people can take them back one day?

Verses 5–6: Memories of Jerusalem
Verses 5 and 6 are, at one level, a protestation of desire to remember Jerusalem:

- Articulate the struggle to remember and remain faithful in the face of temptation to let memory dim. Could be communal way of passing on to the next generation the yearning that arises from dislocation, a reminder that the present arrangements are not right, not to be accepted, that they must not be tempted to assimilate.
- Invoking a curse against failure.
- Countercultural, given that many Jews settled down/assimilated.
- Addresses Jerusalem directly, a feature of some songs of Zion (Psalms 87.3; 122.2, 6–9) – is this a new song of Zion from exile, an attempt to answer their own question?
- To let the right hand wither (v. 5) was devastating for a musician who played a musical instrument.
- Invoked ritual impurity: according to cultic laws being codified at the time, a blemished body prevented priests from leading worship (Leviticus 21.18, 21).
- Tongue clinging to the roof of the mouth (v 6): involuntary silence in contrast to self-imposed silence of vv. 1–3 (cf. Ezekiel 3.26).
- To set Jerusalem above one's highest joy is to adopt a whole orientation to life at odds with life in exile.
- It is to refuse to make a home in Babylon, to live a life of constant unfulfilled longing, refusing to be satisfied with anything less than what seems unattainable at present.
- It is to choose the life of constant remembering and weeping (v. 1).
- It is also to open oneself to the comfort promised for those who mourn in Zion (Isaiah 61.3–4). Perhaps only those

who mourn so deeply can be entrusted with raising up the devastated city (v. 4)?

Verses 7–9: The desire for revenge on Edom and Babylon
Lectionary brackets vv. 7–9 (coyly, lest their inclusion prove offensive to Christian sensibilities?). The historical background is essential for understanding:

- These sentiments can be the outcome of treatment such as that meted out to the people.
    - o Parallels with much terrorism in the world today, which we tend to say is by people who are 'not like us'.
    - o 'The real problem is not that the vengeance is *there* in the Psalms, but that it is *here* in our midst' (Brueggemann) (parallels with Israel, Lebanon, Gaza today). (NB: is this such a powerful emotion that it needs a sermon in itself rather a mention in passing?)
- Verse 7 is the only one in the psalm addressed directly to God who is asked to remember and take action against Edom –
    - o To remember is covenant language (Psalms 74.2, 18; 89.49–50; 119.49; 132.1); takes God and the people back to memory of God's past action and gives hope (Psalm 143.5–6).
    - o Psalmist entrusts revenge to God – cynic could argue he or she was in no position to take revenge into his or her own hands.
    - o Later, Malachi articulated God's perpetual anger with Edom (Malachi 1.2–5) – prayer did not go unanswered.
- 'O daughter Babylon': literally 'daughter of Babylon' and refers to the people of Babylon.
- Verses 8–9 basically a desire for *lex talionis* to operate.
- 'Happy' occurs 26 times in the Psalms;
    - o Other occasions see happiness deriving from relationship with God, or living a godly life.
    - o This suggests that these occurrences are also seen that way: can desire for the defeat of Babylon be godly?

Our discomfort with the general desire that God should act arises from its gruesome specificity – dash the children against the rocks – and because the people appear to relish the prospect: once it was Israel's children who were smashed, now it is to be '*your*' little ones. But:

- Not uncommon for victorious armies to kill children, especially boys; with babies and young children this was often by dashing them against rocks (2 Kings 8.12; Hosea 10.14; 13.16; Nahum 3.10).
- Parallel petitions in Psalms 69.24; 83.10; 109.9–10 and 140.10 plead with God for devastating horrors to befall the enemy – treated as dung for the ground, orphaned and widowed, children forced to beg, driven out of the ruins of their homes, to have burning coals flung on them.
- Not noble sentiments or ones we easily admit to (maybe we need memories of Jerusalem burning to understand?) – What is the ethical response in the face of such horror already done?
- In the previous psalm, killing of the firstborn was cited as an example of the steadfast love of God (Psalm 136.10).
- Dashing children on the rock is born of passion and faith that God will somehow bring an end to this terrible situation: hope is not yet dead and 'It is an act of profound faith to entrust one's most precious hatreds to God, knowing they will be taken seriously' (Brueggemann).

Other thoughts

- Parallels with the story of Samson (Judges 16): uneasy relationship with other nations; taunting and demand for revelation to opponents of something God-given; capture; demand by the captors to be entertained; desire to pay back with an act of revenge.
- Parallels with the 2003 invasion of Iraq: Babylon is about 55 miles south of Baghdad. Saddam Hussein built a palace nearby and tried to rebuild its walls as at the time of Nebuchadnezzar. All that remains now is mud-baked bricks.

Summarizing this exegesis, we are dealing with the thoughts and prayers of people who went through excruciating conditions in Jerusalem, where they nearly starved to death then watched others being butchered; were taken into exile in a land that was in every way alien to them; had all the foundations of their faith and their understanding of God undermined by political events; were humiliated by being forced to perform their sacred songs as entertainment for pagans; found themselves unable to continue doing what they were trained to do and what others looked to them for; had to find a new way to sing the Lord's song if they were not to succumb to doubt and apostasy; and in the midst of their own struggle for faith, had to find ways to keep the painful memory of Jerusalem alive for others and mingle it with hope and joy. In addition they had to acknowledge the burning anger that simmered throughout the years and find a way to deal with it so it did not destroy them. They wanted to remain faithful although it would have been so much easier for them if they didn't. Their answer was to bring the anger to God, to mix it with hope and tears as part of the new way of praying and worshipping that the exile was forging in them. We also have telling connections with contemporary history.

Consider the context of our preaching

Questions to consider may be: What liturgical season is it? Is it a special service? What is the mood of the service? When and where and why will the congregation gather? Who are they – regular worshippers or visitors? What is happening to them? What time of day is it – are people fresh or tired at the end of a working day? Will people be too hot or too cold? How long can they concentrate? What is their sensory experience in the service? Is yours the only voice they will hear? What sermons have these people heard recently? In Christian worship the sermon is part of the bigger whole of the worship of the people of God so we can take some things for granted and do not need to recapitulate the obvious so that people wonder where we have been for the last half hour.

In the case of Psalm 137, there are several potential sermons emerging and decisions will be influenced by the context of the sermon, the identity of the hearers, the local and world situations in which they gather and the liturgical context of the sermon. A congregation hearing Psalm 137 may find personal situations are evoked – adjustment to trauma or long-term changed circumstances over which they are powerless (the onset of long-term illness or disability), loss (through death, redundancy, family moving far away), shattered hopes; or they may be repressing previously unthinkable religious questions about loss of faith and the desire for revenge, or they may be themselves exiles or refugees. With a psalm like this one, world events may be on their mind.

A *few days before: focus and function*

It is wise to avoid trying to do too much in a sermon; some potentially great sermons have to go unpreached each week. Remember Long's two questions: what is the focus of the sermon and what is its function? In other words, what is the key point we want to convey and what do we want people to do as a result of hearing the sermon? If we don't know what we want to do, we are guaranteed to succeed in not achieving it. It is not enough to know that we want to preach on a particular text, we need to be clear what we want the people listening to us to understand and do either while they are still in church or at home. Which of the many powerful themes of Psalm 137 do we want to focus on? For musicians at a choir festival the questions of the first half of the psalm are relevant and the sermon's function may be to help them to think through their role in helping people to keep the faith in hard times, or to sustain their own ministry when they are under pressure; for a congregation soon after a terrorist attack has hit the headlines, the second half may be more relevant with the function of bringing to light our own responses and examining the instinct for revenge, or exploring what lay behind the vindictive thoughts and thus raising questions about whether or not we can appropriate them at face value today.

Once we know the focus, what do we want the sermon to do? We can aim to give information or explain the text, to convert people, to comfort or challenge them, or to win their confidence and thus charm the desired outcome from them. It may be appropriate to preach a sermon that has the deliberate function of teaching or guiding the hearers in order to help them in their ethical lives. This may be the case where a particular issue is troubling the nation or the community. Preachers should not shy away from this when necessary but a regular diet of sermons on moral issues is likely to give a subliminal message that the Christian faith is about little else than a particular moral code.

Style of preaching

Once the focus and function are clearer and thought has been given to the hearers of the sermon, decisions can be made about the most appropriate style of preaching for this sermon, this week. Like those of many new preachers, my early sermons read more like course papers or essays, and I cringe when I look at them; and I've heard more than one professor's sermon that sounded like a lecture. In both cases the wrong written style hindered the spark of communication between preacher and people.

Two crucial considerations are that we must respect the genre of Scripture and we must preach in our own voice, not try to imitate someone else. That does not give us licence to fall automatically into our preferred style, which the congregation may not share. Instead we want to avoid predictability, which dulls our preaching and lulls the congregation into a false sense of security that they know what is coming. Lady Hunstanton's words, given to her by Oscar Wilde, need to ring warning bells:

I am so sorry I was not here to listen to you, I expect I am getting too old to learn now. Except from you, dear Archdeacon, when you are in your nice pulpit. But then I always know what you are going to say, so I am not alarmed.[12]

Styles of preaching in the past should not be discarded simply because they are from the past. Using the language of rhetoric, if we want to appeal to the emotions (*pathos*) of our hearers we should consider the use of story; to appeal to their intellect (*logos*) we might consider argument and appeal to facts; and to build our relationship (*ethos*) with the hearers then we will give particular attention to our delivery.[13] We might then be able to elicit the desired result. Different starting-places can be considered, perhaps starting from a life situation instead of Scripture, or using a narrative approach instead of exposition. Sermons beginning with a question that draws out the meaning of the biblical passage may be more interesting for the listener than one that explains its meaning verse by verse. With dense passages – the first chapters of Ephesians being an example – faceting the passage, taking segments and holding each up to the light as one would a jewel, might be helpful in clearing a path into the riches of the passage. Another approach is to allow the congregation to make discoveries for themselves: take them so far and then let them enjoy coming to new insights or conclusions that they will remember and own.

Used correctly the medium can become (at least in part) the message, but the wrong style of preaching sends confusing signals to the hearers and undermines the message. Whichever style is chosen, even if the preacher is the only person speaking aloud, the congregation are dialogue partners. This is made more explicit in the Godly Play approach of engaging hearers in the dialogue with 'I wonder' questions. It was originally designed for children gathered round a sand tray but can be used successfully when preaching from a pulpit. Careful attention to the way questions are asked is reinforced by pauses that are long enough for people to think about the questions, and this can be hard for preachers who are not comfortable with silence in the pulpit. After I used this approach people commented how helpful it was to have quite demanding questions and silence in the sermon. Here are two extracts from a sermon, one from the middle and one from the conclusion, which worked with the two stories set in the lectionary. The first is the anointing of David by Samuel,

> The Sunday School sometimes uses Godly Play materials which is an approach that works with the children's natural curiosity and imagination, so instead of telling the story the Sunday School helper sits on the floor with the children and together they build the story as the helper asks, 'I wonder what it was like . . .' I'm going to try that with you although this pulpit rather gets in the way of us holding a conversation as would happen in Sunday School. But use your imaginations: imagine yourself as a child standing in front of someone in authority – the head at school perhaps – who surveys you in silence.
>
> I wonder what it was like for Eliab to stand in front of the famous prophet Samuel waiting for him to say something?
>
> I wonder what it was like for Jesse to see his eldest son standing there – pride? confidence?
>
> But then I wonder what it was like for Jesse and his son to hear Samuel say, 'No, not this one'? disappointment? personal affront? confusion? After all, the eldest son was in a privileged position in that culture.
>
> And then the next, and the next, and the next down to the seventh. I wonder what he thought as he was called up, with his six older brothers all rejected?
>
> And still 'No. The Lord has not chosen any of these.' . . .

Later the story of Jesus healing the man born blind was introduced,

> [T]here is the almost comic situation when his parents are called by the religious leaders to explain what is going on. Like the situation with Samuel and Jesse where things don't

add up and perhaps in desperation Samuel asks Jesse 'have you got any more children?', so now the situation is desperate and the parents are wheeled in to see if they can help. But they are at an impasse too: 'This is our son, he was blind, he can see now but we don't know how it happened.' I wonder what it was like for them when there was simply no explanation for what had happened to their son and they as parents couldn't protect him from the fury of the religious authorities? In fact, as the story unfolds, he can argue pretty well but his parents don't know that yet.

And that is where I'm going to leave this sermon, with no neat and tidy ends but more questions that Godly Play might lead us to ponder:

I wonder what it is like to be caught up in the ways of God when we don't understand what is going on?

I wonder what it has been like for you to sense that God is doing something in your life that breaks out beyond what your family or your friends expect of you?

And, on this Mothering Sunday when we've heard two stories where parents find their children being led by God into uncharted territory, I wonder what it is like for all of us – mothers or not – to nurture other people, particularly younger people, in the unexpected ways of God and to free them to respond to the call of God?

Perhaps your Lenten discipline this week can be to let your mind wander into the stories we are hearing week by week and lead you to wonder. Who knows what you will discover?[14]

One style that is best avoided at all costs is the first-person dramatic monologue. Many a Good Friday has been ruined by amateur attempts to get under the skin of people at the crucifixion. However hard we try, we cannot convey what people were thinking or feeling at the time: the Bible doesn't tell us, speculation inevitably sounds hollow and the dramatized result lacks authenticity. If we avoid the first person we can keep some distance between us (the preacher) and the biblical character,

thus opening up a broader canvas to explore. Dramatic monologue is best in the third person because this distance allows
the congregation to imagine the person from the biblical story
and allows what authors call 'the omnipotent voice' to provide insights beyond those of people in the story. Alternatively,
using the second person we can address the person in the story,
perhaps asking them questions.

Drama or mime needs to be well rehearsed to avoid being
amateur. Its impact can be increased by surprise. I used to
complain to my congregation in the USA that I could read
the telephone directory from the pulpit and they'd go out saying, 'Lovely sermon, Vicar', because they were listening to my
British accent. So once I cast myself as the stroppiest sheep
in a drama about the Good Shepherd. It fixed the message in
people's minds both because I'd not used drama before and
because they were shocked I was not the shepherd. Startling
the congregation very occasionally doesn't hurt, so long as the
effect does not detract from the content of the sermon.

PowerPoint rarely belongs in preaching. Apart from the fact
that even brief technical hitches interrupt the encounter of the
sermon, it distances people from the immediacy of oral communication since both preacher and people focus on the screen
rather than each other and thus miss a mutual encounter in the
presence of God. One successful example I experienced was the
projection of just one picture onto a wall (not a screen) from
a concealed projector, which was relevant to the sermon and
enhanced the worship environment: it functioned as art and
served rather than controlled the sermon and the worship.

To return to Psalm 137, what might be an appropriate style
of preaching? It is poetry but it embodies history and ethical
questions. It is a lament and needs to be heard as such, with
its mournful quality, distraught confusion and anger at events
too big to comprehend. It is heavy with memories that need
to be allowed time to surface in the speaker's memory as the
words are spoken. There is a charged undercurrent of emotion
and memory that fills in a lot of blanks unknown to us today
and somehow justifies the sentiments of the last verses which

threaten to overwhelm both speaker and listener. We are over-hearing one speaker's lines in a dialogue with several unknown others – fellow exiles, Jerusalem, perhaps the self, God and Babylon: four or five original addressees in the space of nine verses, and now twenty-first-century listeners too.

This psalm has a story behind it, and that is one way into a sermon that honours the genre of lament psalm in general and this psalm in particular. Unless the historical story is told, the congregation will never be able to grapple with or understand the last verses. If it was spoken by older people to young people there is a certain loss of dignity in admitting, 'We failed, we simply couldn't do this', and the memory the young are being asked to inherit and keep alive is one of honest but seemingly ignominious failure. The only direct address to God comes in verse 7, turning it from mere complaint to lament, and that voice, however muted, must come through in the preaching. It will not be triumphalistic but it will bear witness with quiet confidence that there is a way through this valley of the shadow of death and invite the hearers to follow the shepherd through it.

Even then, there are options. We could introduce the hearers to the way parallelism works and explore avenues that opens up: What insights do the two ways of saying the same thing offer us? 'By the rivers of Babylon – there we sat down and there we wept when we remembered Zion / On the willows there we hung up our harps' are two different responses to one trauma and a sermon could emerge from reflecting with the congregation on the poetic imagery used. The exegetical approach would take it verse by verse and rely heavily on the exegetical discoveries to help people to understand the psalm. The problem here is that it ends with violence and therefore a further step is needed so that people can lay that to rest before moving on from those powerful emotions back into the rest of the liturgy. Therefore something more than exegesis is needed and help towards an appropriate response depends upon the congregation's needs. Another preaching style could be faceting, taking the question 'How could we sing the LORD's song in a foreign land?' and exploring it from different angles. A fourth could be to take a theme – the ministry of music in keeping and passing the faith on to others; surviving when our world collapses around us; the importance of memory. The psalm could also be preached as narrative – telling of exile, despair and anger as story: the ground covered may be similar to that in an exegetical sermon but the result will probably be more vivid. A decision has to be made, and it may be determined by the liturgical context and the expected congregation. It is harder but much more exciting than the old, very structured deductive approaches to preaching.

Notes

1 John Killinger, *Fundamentals of Preaching*, SCM Press, London, 1985, p. 185.

2 That is not to say that we will always then emerge with a sermon in good time, but we will have time to recognize that we are running out of time. See Durham Cathedral Sermons: 28 April 2008, 'Easter, Death and Life', where the admission in the second paragraph that I was bored by my own first attempt at a sermon brought a ripple of laughter.

3 Phillips Brooks, *Lectures on Preaching (1877)*, H. R. Allenson, London, 1895, p. 101.

4 Georges Liébert, *Nietzsche and Music*, trans. David Pellauer, Google Books, accessed 13 April 2009.

5 The *Guardian* newspaper runs a fascinating series of photographs and descriptions of writers' studies – we arrange the physical space in our studies to suit our needs to research and write, but this stage of sermon preparation does not need to be distracted by those tasks.

6 A website like Oremus, http:// bible.oremus.org/ is invaluable. It provides the text of the NRSV and KJV as well as 1662/Coverdale, ASB and Common Worship Psalters.

7 Alan Bennett, *Untold Stories*, Faber & Faber, London, 2005, pp. 547–8.

8 A pericope is a term from biblical criticism and, put very simply, refers to a unit of text that has an element of self-containment about it. The lectionary texts set for a particular day may include more than one pericope.

9 There are several available. I find James Dunn and John Rogerson (eds), *Eerdmans Commentary on the Bible*, Eerdmans, Grand

Rapids and Cambridge, 2003, to be one of the best. Commentaries on the lectionary readings, such as Roger E. van Harn (ed.), *The Lectionary Commentary*, Continuum, London, 2001, are also helpful, but be aware that the Church of England's lectionary differs on a few occasions from the Revised Common Lectionary.

10 This is composite research from several sources done years ago, the notes for which were lost in a trans-Atlantic move, so specific sources cannot be acknowledged.

11 Lucy Dawidowicz, *The War Against the Jews 1933–1945*, Holt, Rinehart & Winston, Austin, TX, 1975 p. 201, quoted in Edward Feld, *The Spirit of Renewal: Finding Faith after the Holocaust*, Jewish Lights Publishing, Woodstock, VT, 1994, p. 90.

12 Lady Hunstanton in Oscar Wilde, *A Woman of No Importance*, Act 3.

13 Charles Denison, *The Artist's Way of Preaching*, Westminster John Knox, Louisville, 2006, p. 11.

14 Durham Cathedral Sermons: 2 March 2008, 'Sons and Parents', Canon Rosalind Brown. See also 11 January 2009, '10:05 and the Baptism of Christ', Canon Stephen Cherry.

9

PREPARING TO PREACH

Finding the Words to Express Our Wonder

A few days before preaching: writing the sermon out

Once decisions are made about content and style, it is time to turn notes into a written text. Remember, this text is not the sermon – that only comes into being when it is preached. New preachers should make an outline first and then fill the text in around it; gradually experience will allow us to go straight into the text. How long should the sermon be? The normal practice in the particular church is important, but so are particular circumstances. My experience of visiting several churches is that Anglicans preach for about 14 minutes, Catholics for slightly less and other Protestant churches for nearer 20 minutes. Preaching at pastoral services is normally under ten minutes. The usual problem is sermons that are too long, either for the congregation's expectations so they become restless, or for the timing of what follows – a Remembrance Day service where the preacher preached on and on, past the 11.00 silence, is unforgettable – but when I preached in South Africa I was told that people would feel they had been short-changed if I preached for less than their (by my standards, long) expected norm. Know how many words you can deliver in a minute and do the calculation every time.

Think of the sermon as a journey for which we are the guide. We have to invite people to come with us, point out scenery en route, encourage their engagement with it and finally bring them safely to a destination that makes the journey worthwhile. Too many sermons simply get lost and thus bore their hearers. There is no excuse for this. So, write out the function and the focus; then, having decided on the style to use, note the key parts and the links between them, noting where things are particularly dense and may need an illustration, or where they are lightweight and could do with more substance. Write out the conclusion to be clear where the sermon is headed, and check that it fulfils the function intended for the sermon. Trace the flow from beginning to end – does it flow naturally or are there sharp turns or even non-sequiturs? Can we keep people with us and interested? Do Scripture and life engage with each other, or is it too heavily weighted towards one or the other? Where is the good news of the kingdom of God? How does it fit with the liturgy? Our aim is a sermon outline that is both clear and interesting: if we are not interested in the subject, how can we hope to inspire others?

Then write the text of the sermon. It is a good discipline, particularly when beginning to preach, to write a full script, since it facilitates systematic preparation, gives an idea of how the material holds together (or does not) and of how long it will take to deliver. It also allows for tight editing to eliminate unnecessary material, note what is missing, see what doesn't ring true, hone the language and practise the delivery. It also helps us to use a wider vocabulary, avoiding the repetition of words for which there are alternatives. Perhaps, above all, it frees us from the anxiety of losing the thread in embarrassed confusion. Most experienced preachers advocate writing the sermon out – Charles Simeon said a preacher's first four hundred sermons should be from a full script[1] and Phillips Brooks, in his Yale lectures on preaching, made a wise observation:

> The real question about a sermon is not whether it is extemporaneous when you deliver it but whether it was ever extemporaneous – whether there was ever a time when the discourse sprang freshly from your heart and mind. The

main difference in sermons is that some sermons are, and others sermons are not, conscious of an audience. The main question about sermons is whether they feel their hearers. If they do they are enthusiastic, personal and warm. If they do not, they are calm, abstract and cold.[2]

Brooks hits on an important point: it is possible to read a script with freshness or to speak without a script and bore everyone into the ground. In past centuries reading a sermon meant just that, the preacher had no eye contact with the congregation. I can remember preachers who appeared to be oblivious of the congregation's presence – one even preached with his eyes closed at times, which was incredibly distracting to look at. It also led to him being unaware of the congregational reaction when his toupee slipped! Pusey apparently was so short-sighted that he had to bend over his notes to read them, but to compensate for this he had mastered the power of oratory and people hung on his every word. He was probably unique in that.

At this stage we are creating a working document. Where do we start? The conclusion is probably the most difficult part to get right, and many experienced preachers advocate writing the conclusion first and then working backwards. The opening is also difficult and may be best left until we know where the rest of the sermon is going. It may be easier to begin writing the sermon just after the beginning. Whatever technique or style we use, get the words on paper in sufficient detail to allow us to edit first the content and then the way we say it.

Starting the sermon

People give us their attention when we enter the pulpit and our task is not to lose it rather than to gain it. We have about one minute to persuade people to stay with us, but they will take a sentence or two to start listening properly so we shouldn't give away our most brilliant line in the first sentence. The introduction is just that, normally no more than a few sentences long it brings people on board so that we can then move forward together. We have lived with the Scriptures and sermon for several days; they have no idea what is coming either in content or starting-point. A dull beginning will test the commitment of even the most dedicated sermon-aficionado; jargon promptly excludes visitors newly putting their toes in the water of church; and a technical beginning will sail over the head of anyone who is not a specialist in that area.

The following introductions to Durham Cathedral sermons work with various possibilities. A colleague began with a verse from one of the readings to set the theme and then immediately alluded to the financial crises that gripped the world in autumn 2008. This juxtaposition of Scripture and world crisis formed the theme of the sermon:

Jesus said to the rich young man, 'If you wish to be perfect, go sell your possessions and give the money to the poor, and you will have treasure in heaven; then come follow me.' (Matthew 19.21)

If, like me, your understanding of banking, commerce and economics is limited, this has been a bewildering week. But I understand that if you are expert in banking, commerce and economics the week has been just as bewildering. Strange things have been going on in the world of international finance. Recent financial events have rocked the system and caused people to wonder about the big picture and worry about their own financial security. We had a foretaste of this with the Northern Rock crisis and there is something profoundly unsettling when people begin to be actively concerned that their savings are safe, their investments secure, whether their home will be repossessed and if their job is vulnerable.[3]

The next, very visual, opening drew out imaginative and humorous possibilities within the Scripture, before turning to address more serious issues. It invited people to imagine the scene through an unexpected lens, and the sermon then explored God's presence with us in confined places, before ending with the image from the introduction of angels tapping us on the side and asking us to follow them:

> Every organization has its funny stories which it retells over the years, and I suspect we heard one from the early church today. I hope Rhoda had a good sense of humour because I expect she got fed up hearing, 'Do you remember when Peter got out of prison but was left hammering on the door because Rhoda forgot to open it?' I can also imagine Charlie Chaplin acting this entire episode in one of his silent films – sleeping in prison between the soldiers, being tapped on the side by an angel (what an evocative phrase that is; it is not the usual form of greeting from an angel in the Bible), waking up and fumbling to get his clothes on, looking behind him to see the soldiers still sleeping, being abandoned in the street, knocking on the door of the house and being unable to get the church to open it. It was easier for Peter to escape from prison than to get into church. There is something gloriously humorous about the whole thing.
>
> But there is also something very serious.[4]

In the next introduction a theme within the Gospel reading set the overall frame for the sermon, but the question asked in the introduction was then suspended until mid-way through the sermon to allow exploration of the Gospel reading. It was then revisited before being left again for further exploration of Scripture and finally was picked up to shape the conclusion:

> Twice in today's readings things happen suddenly to Jesus: suddenly a leader of the synagogue came in; suddenly a woman came up behind him. Matthew doesn't use 'suddenly' very often in his Gospel, it's more a word you'd expect to find in Mark and where Matthew does use it, it is in the context of heaven and earth colliding in some way – angels have a habit of suddenly appearing: to the wise men after they had been to see the infant Jesus, to Jesus in the wilderness

after his temptations; or God acts suddenly and decisively: at the transfiguration, in an earthquake when the women went to the tomb and soon after when Jesus suddenly appeared to them; or demons react suddenly in the events just before today's Gospel reading when Jesus heals two demoniacs. The two occurrences of the word 'suddenly' in the stories we heard today are unusual because, on the face of it, there is nothing untoward about the events: Jesus is doing one thing – talking to John's disciples or walking with people – when someone else appears. That happens often enough in every-day life, so why does Matthew use the word 'suddenly' to describe the encounters?

Hold that question for a while.[5]

This introduction began from an event that was known to several people but needed explanation for visitors. Preached in the Easter season, the sad death opened the window on the resurrection hope:

A few weeks ago, I represented this Cathedral at the funeral of Bishop Kevin Dunn, Roman Catholic Bishop of Hexham and Newcastle, at St Mary's Cathedral in Newcastle. Bishop Kevin died at the age of 57, having been bishop for only a few years; it was a poignant and moving occasion. But I was particularly struck by the conclusion to the sermon preached by Archbishop Vincent Nichols of Birmingham, the diocese from which Bishop Kevin had come to Newcastle. The Gospel at the funeral Mass was the account of the raising of Lazarus from St John's Gospel. Archbishop Nichols talked of having visited Kevin Dunn and seeing all the tubes, lines and appliances that were sustaining him up to the end of his life. So the conclusion to the Gospel reading had special poignancy, 'Unbind him, and let him go free.'

'Unbind him and let him go free.' For to all of us who share an Easter faith, death is not the disaster that it seems to be to so many people in our generation. It is not hopeless. And hopeless death is growing in our society.[6]

This introduction sets up the theme of the sermon, the story of Thomas, but alerted people to the fact that this was not simply a biography by creating an interesting tension – Thomas was an individual but also a twin:

> My favourite moment in the film, *The Life of Brian*, is where Brian is trying to get rid of the crowd and so he tells them that they are all individuals. 'Yes', they chorus back, 'We are all individuals.' 'You are all different' Brian calls back. 'Yes, we are all different', they reply.
>
> Unlike the members of this crowd, Thomas *was* an individual, Thomas was different. He was not in the upper room on the first occasion. We do not know why but it made him a bit different, the odd one out. And earlier in the Gospel after the raising of Lazarus it was Thomas who said, 'let us go with Jesus so that we might die with him'. He was unique in saying this. As I heard someone once say when he stumbled across this line for the first time: 'It tells you a different story about Thomas.' Indeed it does.
>
> Thomas the individual, then. But that's an odd thing to say because John tells us that Thomas is a twin.[7]

This sermon introduction began a Palm Sunday sermon. The vivid illustration of Jesus in a supermarket trolley could have upstaged the whole sermon had the preacher not immediately used it to make an unexpected link to daily life, which set the tone for the rest of the sermon about Jesus' humility:

> We cannot help but read this verse through our memories of processions with palm crosses within around or to parish churches or cathedrals. Personally I have a surprisingly rich set of Palm Sunday memories. I was in Cape Town one year and remember the baking heat as the guitar-playing priest led the congregation around the desolate area called District Six – a once thriving multi-ethnic community that was razed to the ground in the apartheid years. Only the church, the mosque remained, and yet the congregation of former

residents continued together at St Mark's. Later that day, I attended what was billed as a 'passion play' at a church on the Cape Flats. This was a compilation of songs from *Godspell* and *Jesus Christ Superstar* performed by the church choir. The choirmaster and organist, a very large man, cast himself as Jesus. When it came to the Palm Sunday scene this Jesus was propelled on to the stage in a supermarket trolley. No one, including this Jesus, could keep a straight face. But it said something about Jesus and the ordinary everyday things of life.[8]

This sermon began vividly in the Old Testament reading and summarized the story very succinctly before exploring it and allowing Hannah to have her own voice. Because the readings were controlling the sermon, it was Zechariah rather than the perhaps more predictable Mary, who joined the dialogue later in the sermon. The liturgical setting was a strong background factor – it was two days before Christmas and the conclusion acknowledged what the congregation had known all along but did not need to be told, that the themes that had been explored are particularly relevant in the Christmas season:

> Poor childless Hannah, scorned by her prolific rival in marriage, Penninah with all her sons and daughters. 'For the Lord had closed her womb.' In ancient society, a marriage without children was not simply a disappointment: it was a failure. Women like Sarah, Abraham's wife, Michal, David's wife, and Hannah the wife of Elkanah were destined to go through life at best pitied, more often mocked and despised for their infertility. It's a terrible word the Bible uses – *barrenness*. Her husband, one of the best men in the Old Testament, tries to comfort her: 'Why is your heart sad? Am I not more to you than ten sons?', surely one of the most beautiful sayings in the Old Testament. But Hannah knows where to take her distress. She goes to the sanctuary, where she makes a vow that if the Lord grants her desire, the child will be offered to him for ever. Pouring out her grief pro-

duces catharsis. 'The woman went to her quarters, ate and drank with her husband, and her countenance was sad no longer . . .' Hannah conceives, and bears a son, who is given back to God. He will be the first of the long line of Hebrew prophets. His name is Samuel.[9]

The final sermon introduction, at the poignant final attendance at a Cathedral service by the City Council, just prior to its politically contentious abolition, began by setting the occasion in a historical context that, as the sermon developed, was shown to be able to contain the present ambivalent experience in a longer, stable historical tradition. It used local history to reframe this event within the Christian tradition. By doing this, the whole mood of the abolition was subtly shifted towards hope that this event could become part of Durham's living tradition, and by doing this the sermon offered profound pastoral ministry at a civic service.

'This was surrender in a grand manner, both abject and comprehensive, leaving not the smallest loophole through which a lawyer might wriggle at any time in the future to argue and obtain alteration.' That is not a report on the dissolution of district councils in Durham and Northumberland, but an historian's comment on a dissolution of earlier times when this institution we are now sitting in came to the end of an era. It is chronicled in Geoffrey Moorhouse's book about Durham, *The Last Office: 1539 and the Dissolution of a Monastery*. The consequences of a royal whim to reorganize the nation's polity arrived for good in Durham on the last day of that year. That night Prior Hugh Whitehead led his monks into this church for the last time to recite the ancient office of compline. The psalms finished, they came to a poignant *Nunc Dimittis*: 'Now lettest thou thy servant depart in peace; for mine eyes have seen thy salvation.' It is the canticle of leave-taking and death. And this was a kind of death. When the sound of plainchant died away on that new year's eve, something died with it – five centuries of common life and prayer here that this church would never see again in that form.

This service of leave-taking may be bewildering for some of you, and poignant for many more. The City Council has not been a feature of Durham life for as long as the Priory was, but that does not mean that its dissolution is not deeply felt, at least by those who have given many years to it as elected members, officers and employees. Perhaps the memory that this church has been there before could be important. The re-engineering of institutions is hard because of the memories we carry but especially when an institution is there for 'public benefit'. The Cathedral Priory existed to serve God and the community. No doubt it did not always live up to that high Benedictine ideal but that was not given as a reason for dissolving it. In the same way, Durham City Council has served this city with an energy and distinction that have brought it credit. It comes to an end because government has decreed that things are to be done differently. Whatever our regrets, it is emphatically not a matter of failure or shame. We should celebrate success and give thanks for our achievements, hard though it may be to do today.[10]

To go back to Psalm 137, how might that sermon start? One effective possibility (which I used) is to learn the psalm and pray it from the pulpit with appropriate emotion (practise hard beforehand and try out alternative emphases). It brings the power of the words home but, if that sounds too risky, there are more conventional ways in. I am writing this a few months into the global financial crisis that has given all-too-real meaning to the term 'credit crunch' for nations and individuals. People are living with insecurity in a way that was inconceivable even a few months ago, so one starting-point could be:

You don't need me to tell you that we are living in uncertain economic times, and insecurity is all too familiar. It's all very biblical! In times of prosperity in the Bible there was no need for people to deal with their anger (in fact the prophet

Amos tells us that instead that was *God's* problem with them because of their indifference to the distress of others). But, as we heard in the psalm, when crisis struck, their anger and desire for revenge were exposed and had to become part of their relationship with God. That was a challenge for them and is a challenge for us: it is so much easier when disaster strikes to blame it on God or to say that it is proof God does not exist. But how can we be faithful to God without denying the questions and emotions that trauma brings? In the words of the psalm, 'How can we sing the LORD's song in a foreign land?'

An alternative approach that would take the sermon in a different direction is to begin with the silenced singers,

Sometimes we hear of children who simply refuse to speak and it takes the skill of counsellors and psychiatrists to get them talking again. Those services were not available to the singers we heard about in the psalm who, when things got too much to bear, simply stopped singing. They hung up their harps and wanted their tongues to stick to the roofs of their mouths because there was no way they could go on singing when their captors taunted and mocked them, demanding to be entertained by songs about their holy God. They could not cope with what was happening so chose silence for their safety net. We, who have no idea of what trauma they faced, can't blame them.

These were the people who had sung in the temple, leading people in worship. The faith of others would suffer as a result of their actions because they carried the tradition and passed it on to the next generations. What would we do if our choir suddenly said that they can no longer sing, not because they don't want to but because it is just too painful to be mocked as they sing words of faith? Centuries of tradition would die.

What can we do when we feel we have no alternative but to give up, when tradition is extinguished in an instant?

Developing the sermon

The chosen style of preaching affects the way its focus is developed and the overview of the history of homiletics in Chapter 2 outlined many of the options. However we develop the sermon, we move within the framework of the Christian faith, since this is a sermon in the context of worship. That does not mean that every statement we make is backed up by a reference to Scripture or the creeds, but it does mean that we are faithful to their presence in the background. The aim is for a flowing movement in content and delivery, with rhythm in speech that is neither sing-song nor jarring. Weak content or weak delivery will cause the sermon to crash: in a scathing comment Jonathan Raban said of President Clinton's inaugural speech, 'Words that were already dead on the page died a second death as Clinton gave them voice.'[11] People switch off when they lose confidence in a speaker or the thread of the speech, so, to keep people with us, moves should be made gradually and carefully. While people want to hear something of substance, few are used to hearing long speeches – students take notes in lectures and that physical action helps concentration, whereas our hearers are sitting still, perhaps on hard pews. So we must help them to listen and to become theologians who think theologically; to become prophets who think and act prophetically; to be caring and compassionate in their daily lives. Someone who is caring day in, day out, for a demanding relative faces the same serious questions about God, justice, suffering, compassion and burnout as a political activist, and we can help all of them to think and act theologically through a sermon that engages attention and moves beyond general platitudes.

It is now rare for a sermon to state both theme and thesis at the beginning and then proceed to prove it, reaching an absolutely predictable conclusion. Recalling how Buttrick's moves are carefully made and linked, now the art is to introduce our theme and thesis without giving all our moves away; too many preachers give the punchline away too quickly, and we shouldn't be afraid to keep the congregation in suspense for a while. It is not the same as catching people out, and if we startle people with a punchline that comes out of the blue they will lose their bearings. For help with this, listen to how comedians tell jokes. If we make the central thesis the climax of the sermon, the content should lead up to it so that the congregation arrives at the same conclusion for themselves just when we do and they will remember because it is their discovery. If the central thought is a new or complex one, revealing it at the end may leave people floundering whereas putting it in the middle allows us to lead people towards it and then help them assimilate it. If so, the second part of the sermon needs to maintain the momentum rather than fade away.

Some options for developing the sermon include exploring the theme through biblical exegesis and Christian writings,[12] staying close to the biblical text and exploring its meaning or its example to us,[13] setting the biblical material in historical context and drawing parallels with contemporary situations,[14] running the biblical material alongside another story, letting one inform the other,[15] telling the story of a saint and exploring how we can learn from or emulate his or her example in our day,[16] amplifying an aspect of Christian doctrine before suggesting application for today[17] or recounting our own experience in order to illustrate the theme.[18]

As already indicated, a sermon on Psalm 137 could go in many directions. Faced with the desolation of the original psalmist, which could end up dominating what people hear, perhaps help for the preacher lies in the stubborn determination not to succumb to hopelessness but to keep memory alive and carve out a new way to pass on the heritage of faith and hope, even to mention the word 'joy' in the midst of sorrow. Developing a sermon that honours the genre of poetic lament but does not abandon people could involve passing on the story behind the psalm and letting the congregation feel the burden and impasse of the psalmist for themselves before moving on, in a pastoral and gently prophetic mode, to interpret verses 5–6 as the answer to the question in verse 4: 'How could we do it? This is how . . .' If this approach is taken then either verses 7–9 are part of the new song of Zion, or the psalmist stops the song of Zion at the end of verse 6 and addresses the Babylonians who were referred to in verse 3. Depending on which interpretation is chosen, the sermon will continue in a more pastoral or a more prophetic vein. Another approach could be to treat verses 5–6 as the personal musings of an elderly person lost in their thoughts that then give way to the imprecation of verses 7–9 as the God of Jerusalem is invoked, in which case the preacher might come alongside the psalmist and even address them in the second person along the lines of the example of my address to Mary at the foot of the cross.

Coming to a stop

We have all heard sermons that appear to end but, to our dismay, restart. Heed the King's advice to the White Rabbit in *Alice In Wonderland* about giving evidence: 'Begin at the beginning, and go on till you come to the end: then stop.'[19] Stopping is sometimes easier said than done. If one danger is simply evaporating, leaving everyone abandoned and unsure of their bearings (vividly described as leaving an impression like the delta of the Mississippi which sprawls away instead of coming to a clear destination[20]), the other is stopping abruptly: just as in driving, do not slam on the brakes, because people will hit the windscreen. Work towards the conclusion (only saying 'finally' when it really is finally) and notice how other preachers give subliminal hints that they are coming to their conclusion so that hearers unconsciously pace themselves towards the finish. If we need to pull the threads together, avoid recapping the whole sermon and do not take people back to where we started because the sermon is not a circular ramble but a journey to a new destination; if we want them to remember one thing in particular, revisit it briefly but in a different way from our earlier approach.

New ideas should never be introduced in conclusions and, at this stage, avoid quotations in a different voice from our own unless they are very brief and very apposite; it is jarring for hearers who are readying themselves to finish. Even the best sermon loses momentum if it concludes with a long passage of Scripture; if Scripture is essential at this point, we should summarize it briefly in our own words unless it is a readily recognizable text. Asking questions at the end of the sermon is tempting, but the accumulated wisdom is that this is a bad idea and reduces the impact (particularly if there is no pause for silent reflection after the preacher finishes speaking, something that should be an integral part of the sermon). Don't fizzle out either in content or volume; end with power but not with noise and leave people with an idea ringing in their ears or a picture painted in their imaginations. In the context of the Eucharist, the double focus to this liturgy means it is a valid purpose for the sermon to lead people towards the liturgy of the sacrament and encourage them to 'draw near with faith', entrusting the outcome of our preaching to our Lord who has promised to be with us whenever we 'do this in remembrance of me'.

The following endings from sermons preached in Durham Cathedral illustrate a range of possibilities. Sometimes the preceding paragraph is included to show the move from the substance of the sermon to the conclusion. In the first, on the stoning of Stephen, the penultimate paragraph brought together themes from the sermon before the conclusion applied them and pointed forward to the eucharistic celebration:

But we can't abandon Saul, the young man with the desire for the blood of his enemies, just as I can't forget the violence of the stabbing incident I got involved in. The Bible does not prettify Saul's past just because he becomes a hero in the future. Easter is about new life coming out of death, and Saul is clearly dead wrong at the time of Stephen's death: his religious zeal may be sincere but it is totally misdirected. Only the gospel of resurrection can free Saul from his spiritual death and reframe his actions. For me, in the days after Maundy Thursday last year, that incident and the whole passion story as it unfolded until Easter Day reframed each other and I was given new insights by the juxtaposition of experiences of violence, a wound in a man's side, blood, onlookers and human vulnerability.

This Easter – and it is still Easter – the challenge we face is to let the story of Stephen's horrific death belong with the comfort that Jesus offered his disciples before he died. The only way I know to reconcile the two, and to let each add profound depth to the other, is to see them both through the lens of the death and resurrection of Jesus, and the disturbing comfort that brings. How else can we hold together life and death in our own stories or the stories we hear in the news? On the same day I heard the choir sing that anthem, I heard of the birth of a new baby to members of this congregation and the death of someone who has served this Cathedral for about 40 years through her skills in embroidery. How else can we hold together the joy of Lucy's new life and the sadness of Hilda's death? How else but to say, with profound Easter conviction, 'If we believe that Jesus died and rose again, ev'n so them also which sleep in Jesus will God bring with him. Wherefore comfort one another with these words.' Or, as we will affirm in our celebration of the Eucharist in a few minutes, 'Alleluia. Christ our Passover is sacrificed for us. Therefore let us keep the feast. Alleluia.'[21]

The next sermon followed the same approach and is an example of strong liturgical preaching. The penultimate paragraph drew the threads of the sermon together before the final paragraph linked the congregation back to the Old Testament Scripture and invited them to live into it through the liturgy. The context was Easter Day when the faithful response is joyful worship:

Easter faith invites us to believe that our destiny lies not with the great and powerful of this world, whether they be cruel or benign, but with the one who is risen from the dead, whose kingdom is righteousness and peace, whose power is love poured out. It's not to Ozymandias but to Jesus Christ risen and ascended that the honorific belongs, 'king of kings'. It takes a leap of the imagination to think that this could be true. Everything seems to speak against it: the pain and suffering that surround us, the abuses of power and the threat of terror that are the staple of each day's news, economic crisis and climate change, the unstoppable rise of secularism in our society. Yet it took a leap of the imagination for Mary Magdalen to believe that the one she had supposed to be the gardener was none other than the risen Jesus who ascends to reign with his Father and will one day come in glory on the clouds of heaven. We are always, perhaps, hoping against hope, and never more than on Easter Day.

Yet Easter announces that the promised end of the story we long for is already present in its humble beginnings. Resurrection happens in a garden, like the garden of Eden where the first man was given life. The light dawns on the first day of the week, like the first day of creation when light sprang out of darkness. The message is: the new creation has begun. Today we celebrate how 'the kingdoms of the world have become the kingdom of our Lord and of his Christ, and he will reign for ever and ever'. We acclaim this festival day as the day the Lord has made, a day of glory and victory. It is our Exodus, our deliverance, our promise of new beginnings and hope without end. So we make the song of Moses and the Israelites our own and sing with them: 'The Lord is my strength and my might, and he has become my salvation. This is my God and I will praise him.'[22]

In this Palm Sunday sermon on humility, the preacher had a short conclusion in terms of our own response which followed from a longer summary of tensions within the Scripture and our cultural understandings of what it means to be humble:

Another reason why people can't quite think of Jesus' entry as humble is because of what happens next. He goes into the Temple and lets fly. My Bible has the subheading 'Jesus cleanses the Temple'. 'Makes a mess of it' would be nearer the mark. Turning over the tables and shouting. Again not the sort of behaviour we expect of the humble. Humble people are not confrontational. It is the arrogant and conceited who act out of that sort of passion.

Or is it? Maybe the point of Palm Sunday is to help us understand that humility and self-presentation, humility and passion can indeed be deeply and profoundly connected. In a dictionary article about humility the author writes that 'In contemporary Western cultures, often described as narcissistic and prone to self-delusion, humility has been marginalized.' I think this is profoundly true. We live in a humility-averse culture. We do not trust anything to do with humility. I blame Charles Dickens for creating the unctuous Uriah Heep.

But Jesus' entry into Jerusalem is the opposite of his cloying, manipulative self-description as 'umble'. It is assertive and bold, it is energizing and empowering, and it is all of a piece with the passion, truth and vulnerability that is revealed in the Temple.

Jesus' entry is indeed a humble entry. Maybe if we can learn how to see it in that way we might begin to rehabilitate the values and truth that are enshrined in that modest and yet deeply distrusted, uncommon and yet fundamental Christian word, 'humility'.[23]

A sermon preached two days before Christmas set the story of Hannah, one of the readings for the day, alongside the themes of the liturgical season and the stories surrounding the incarnation. The move to the conclusion was hinted at in the penultimate paragraph and made in the final one. The last sentence quoted, without saying that it was doing so, a hymn that may have rung bells for the congregation:

Monarchy, empire and glory must have been a long way from Hannah's mind when she wept tears of frustration in the sanctuary that day. She simply 'asked for' a child, but what she 'asked for' changed Israel's history. Perhaps it was similar for Zechariah. How could he have conceived that what took place in the temple would lead to the overturning of the world's history? How could he have guessed that it pointed to a different kind of monarchy, empire and glory, what our second reading from Revelation describes as a new heaven and a new earth. For Hannah, for Mary, there was an undreamed, unglimpsed future enfolded in the divine promise of motherhood. So much hangs on such a slender thread.

How can we ever know what our own 'yes' to God may lead to? What matters is to say it in humility and hope, entrust the outcome to God, and go on living and working in the best way we can as we bear witness to the promise of what is yet to come. The name Hannah means 'grace', and grace means gift. In this holy season we see the glory of the only-begotten Son, full of grace and truth. In him, we are truly *heard*, for he is all that we could ever *ask for*, the fulfilment of all our hungers and desires. In him, the thing prayed for does not come short of the prayer, for where expectation meets reality, hope is emptied in delight.[24]

In the next example the bulk of the sermon was devoted to the familiar story of Daniel in the lion's den, but four paragraphs from the end drew in the other reading, the parable of the sower. Rather than hammer home the 'meanings' of the different type of soil, the reasonable assumption was made that we want to be faithful disciples and the conclusion took that readiness and asked what it meant in this particular liturgical season. The congregation was encouraged to let the two familiar stories and the liturgical season rub up against each other in their lives and were given a way to express this in lines from the hymn that was to follow:

And so Daniel's story, linked to the parable, challenges us with what it costs us to say – as I hope we still do – that of course we want to be good soil, not rocky, thistly or shallow soil that is useless for crop bearing. But perhaps the rocks and thistles seem a little more attractive when we consider the cost of being planted in good soil.

We're in the month between All Saints Day and Advent when we do a lot of remembering, as Canon Kennedy reminded us a couple of weeks ago. We remember the saints, all the faithful departed, the fifth of November, the millions who have died or been injured in war, and Hild, Margaret and Archbishop Langley among our local saints. We've also remembered the recent tragic deaths of four brave fire fighters in this country, and the victims of various terrorist attacks around the world. They all knew the cost of commitment to a cause, and their stories could also contribute to the dialogue with the dangerously familiar parable of the sower, the seed and the soil.

Remember Jesus' words when he told the story: let anyone with ears, listen. Don't think you know the story already. Listen today to the parable and to Daniel, let him tell us what the parable is about in practice. If we want to bear good crops we must be ready for the challenges that come, as they did for Daniel, in the midst of daily work and daily life. Listen too to the stories of the people we are remembering in this season. Then can we sing confidently with Daniel and with them of the streams of living waters springing from eternal love that well supply God's sons and daughters and all fear of want remove.[25]

A sermon that had explored the Cathedral's Lenten theme 'Being Human', in the light of the Old Testament lectionary reading and an experience in Soweto, drew several threads together and at the very end introduced the resurrection hope of the New Testament reading before leaving people with the challenge to find ways to reflect that Christian hope in their daily living.

So, at the start of Lent, what do our readings tell us about what it is it to be human?

To be human is to be created in God's image, to be entrusted with the care of God's world, to have freedom to explore all aspects of it – what a wonderful licence for scien-

tific research that is in this year when we remember Darwin
– but it is also to face boundaries put there for our own
good, and to be limited by death. It involves taking responsibility for our actions but also for knowing and caring about
the injustices and inequities in this world because people are
vulnerable, even gullible, and willing to exploit others in their
greed for instant gratification. The world economic crisis is
forcing us to face these truths about ourselves and the whole
world seems to be trying to blame someone else. That's no
surprise, it's all there in Genesis when Adam blamed Eve
and Eve blamed the serpent: *plus ça change*. Perhaps Lent
is a time for being accountable ourselves in areas of our life
where we'd rather abdicate responsibility.

But, finally and gloriously, being human is forever determined by the fact that Jesus Christ, the Second Person of the
Trinity, the Second Adam, has conquered death which is the
consequence of sin, and opened to us the gate of glory. To be
human is to be capable of transformation. For that, thanks
be to God.

In the light of all this, and bearing in mind the power of
story to embody theological insights, what do our lives show
of what it is to be human? What would it be like if, this Lent,
we were all more conscious of our humanity? What simple
actions of living for good can we do today, this week, to
show humanity in its true light in Jesus Christ?[26]

The final example of a sermon ending was preached in the
liturgical context of Mozart's Requiem Mass on All Souls
Day. The congregation had heard Mark's seemingly unfinished
Gospel, ending with the fear of the women as they fled from the
shockingly empty tomb; in the sermon this was set alongside
Mozart's unfinished Requiem and in particular its 'Lacrimosa',
which was the last music he ever composed:

In other words, Mark tells a story we all recognize: how our
lives as people of faith are lived between the cross and the
empty tomb behind us, and the promise of a future with the

risen Lord ahead. We are like the women: we have looked into the face of death and its aftermath, and confronted with its mystery, we are filled with fear. *Dies irae, dies illa solvet saeclum in favilla* – underneath the imagery of that great sequence, we recognize the dread we all feel at our own mortality and what lies beyond. Perhaps it is better to think that we shall lie in the dust forever than that this earth may one day dissolve in ashes and humanity have a future we cannot glimpse or comprehend. Yet what Mark's story holds out to us is hope: the promise that what bewilders and frightens us will one day dissolve in delight. One day. Not now, not yet. It lies in the future. For now, we still live in the shadow of death. But not always. We shall meet him, and greet him and bless him; and then we shall understand.

Like Mozart, Mark laid down his pen to the sombre tones of his own 'Lacrimosa'. But this is not any lack of faith on his part. For the Easter story is always unfinished, always open-ended; resurrection is the beginning not the end, the dawn of a new day whose course is beyond our imagining, though not our hoping. Our lives now are suspended between grave and Galilee, between tearful farewells and joyous reunions, between the emptiness of death and the fullness of life and peace. We come here afraid yet hopeful, discomfited yet believing. 'He goes before you: there you will see him.' The 'Lacrimosa', in the key of D minor, ends on a major chord – Mozart's last. Out of the agonized depths of 'Lacrimosa' comes the text of peace: 'Sweet Lord Jesus, grant them rest. *Pie Jesu Domine, dona eis requiem*'. It isn't yet the happy ending where death is swallowed up in victory. But it foreshadows it. And because of it, we pray for all whom we remember tonight, and know that we are heard.[27]

Illustrations

Illustrations can help to make the message clear and add interest to the sermon, making it memorable and translatable into action. Most sermons, except those where the biblical text is already very vivid and memorable – Psalm 137 being a classic example – benefit from appropriate illustrations. Having a fairly firm idea of the content of the sermon a few days before it is preached gives time to find the right illustration.

Why use illustrations? Theologically, we believe in the incarnation, that God in Christ has known the specificity of life in first-century Palestine. The Bible is full of stories of God's engagement with the people, both of Israel and the surrounding nations. So to preach biblically we must preach with specifics. Practically, illustrations that paint mental pictures through images and stories are more memorable for listeners than abstract ideas; we can imagine something as big 'as a football pitch' but not visualize it from precise dimensions, and we can understand the peace of God better if is described in practice than in theory. It's the Eliza Doolittle principle: 'Don't talk of love, show me!' Illustrations help us to remember things but if they are extraneous or overwhelming – off-colour jokes or heart-rending stories, for example – we remember the illustration not the point it serves. I remember a preacher labouring for half a sermon to describe the complex story of a book which illustrated a point in his sermon – years later I can tell you about the book but have no idea of the sermon content. More vividly, a member of the congregation, on hearing I was writing this book, said that the best sermon she ever heard was as a child at a harvest festival. The preacher took a tomato into the pulpit and rammed his fist down on it. I enquired about the message of that action and she admitted that she had no idea but, interestingly, described it as the best sermon not the best illustration. When I asked my most recent group of students about sermons they remember, every one of them spoke of a sermon where the delivery or the illustration made the overall sermon memorable for good or ill.

Illustrations need to fit the content and form of the sermon within the liturgy, rather than stand out like a sore thumb because they have a very different structure or emotional feel from the rest of the sermon or are so unrelated to the sermon content that hearers have to make an enormous mental leap to grasp them. Check that they can't be misunderstood or read in more than one way. Recently I switched off a recording of an evangelistic sermon by a well-known preacher because there were interminable stories but no substance or sense of direction. Normally two illustrations are ample for any sermon and frequently one is enough; and aim for simplicity and conciseness, since they are the servants not the focus of the sermon. Use a wide range of sources and types of illustrations: if we always use the same source (books, films, sport) people who do not share that interest will miss the point. Occasionally review the cumulative effect of illustrations for bias. If we offend people with inappropriate or bizarre illustrations we have lost them for good, and contentious subjects like abortion or euthanasia need a sermon in their own right; as illustrations they distract the congregation by evoking a strong response. Trite, too-good-to-be-true or obviously artificial stories make people groan inwardly. Humour can be appropriate or detract from a serious theme and it should never be off-colour or at someone's expense. Children are entitled to privacy, and stories involving them are more useful as examples of ordinary life than as examples to follow. Never breach confidence and only name people if we have their permission or the story is about a public figure and is already in the public domain.

Quotations in sermons need care. We are preaching with our own authority and should have the courage of our convictions, but a quotation may say things better. However, it will not be in our speech pattern and therefore will jar, so, if the quotation can't be rephrased in our own words, keep it very short (even two sentences may be too much) and use it early on in the sermon. Only attribute a quotation when speaking if the person is very well known, otherwise say 'someone has said . . .', because citing an unknown name will sound like a footnote in an academic book. There is, though, a fine line between that and plagiarism, so if the sermon appears in written form (on the web, for example), add a footnote citing the source. The same applies if we lift content from someone else's sermon on the web – it is plagiarism to claim their words for our own.[28] Apart from the ethical questions, it suggests that there has been no exegesis of the congregation or crafting of a sermon to meet their needs.

Poetry is difficult to use in sermons. It can be hard to grasp on one hearing and, by its nature, tends to leave things open-ended. However, a couple of well-chosen lines from a great poet can express something far more eloquently and evocatively than our prose. Hymns can work in sermons because they already belong in the context of worship and are associated with a tune that aids memory and identification.

Where do we place illustrations? There are various possibilities. At the beginning they can set the context for what we want to say; in the middle they can reinforce or amplify a point, revive flagging concentration or help to shift the focus; at the end an apt illustration can help to bring threads together and say, 'This is how what I have been speaking about can look in daily life.' Try moving an illustration around because the same illustration will work differently at different places. Once we have it where we think it is most appropriate, try it out for preachability: does it ring true as we tell it, or are the words not our own? If necessary rewrite it or abandon it altogether. The acid test of whether it is likely to work is to ask, 'When people go home, what will they remember?' If it is the illustration alone it has upstaged the sermon as a whole.

A final word about books of canned illustrations: they are anathema! They never work because they sound trite and do not come from the life of the preacher or the congregation. Even worse are canned sermons: in the USA I received regular fliers and one had the nerve to say, 'Because you are a busy pastor, we'll send you two ready-made sermons each week so that you don't have to write your own . . .' If we rely on second-hand material from people writing generically we are, quite simply, not being shepherds to our people. The corollary to that is that we should always be on the alert for and recording potential material so we can draw on it when needed. Life is full of rich resources, it is part of our vocation as preachers to be attentive to life. The best illustrations are nearly always local to the congregation, because they reflect their context: so read the local paper, listen to the radio, watch local life – wondering imagination is essential!

Editing the sermon

'Stickiness' has been described as what makes some ideas stick in the mind while others don't.[29] Editing is vital to achieve stickiness and can make all the difference between a pedestrian sermon and one that lives and breathes. It can be exhilarating to bring a sermon to life, so think of it as crafting and approach editing with enthusiasm: it can only get better! It may help to leave the sermon for a day and then imagine ourselves hearing it for the first and only time. Be honest: do I want to listen to it? Does it stick to the focus? If not, is it the sermon or the focus that needs to be amended? Does it fulfil its function? What is the balance of Scripture, theology, and illustration? Is it all in the right order? Do we need to build in pauses, either to identify a shift in thought or to let what we have said sink in before moving on? Is there energy in it? Shakespeare said that 'brevity is the soul of wit',[30] and it is also the soul of a good sermon: conciseness sharpens it and creates energy, so be totally ruthless and omit anything that is not necessary.

Once we are happy with the content of the sermon it is time to tackle the language.[31] Go through it with a fine-tooth comb and eliminate all words and phrases that deaden it. Bland words – 'that', 'which', 'it', 'this', 'would', 'those' – are prime candidates for extinction, as are 'very', 'only', 'truly' 'really' and 'just'. Clichés, jargon and slang should go. Look at the tenses: when telling a story, use the present rather than the past tense to bring Jesus' actions into the present as the live events that they are in the encounter of preaching: 'Jesus looks at Zacchaeus and says, "What are you doing in that tree when I want to come to have dinner with you?"' rather than 'Jesus walked over to the tree and told Zacchaeus he wanted to eat with him that evening.' Direct rather than indirect speech and the active rather than the passive voice give immediacy ('"I'll find the page," she said, and opened the Bible' rather than 'The Bible was opened and she said she would find the page') and metaphors are more vivid than comparisons: Jesus said, 'I am the vine, you are the branches' not 'I am like a vine and you are like the branches.'

Owl in *Winnie the Pooh* liked long words but thereby confused his audience. So cut out extraneous and long words if a shorter word is available with the same meaning: Charles Wesley may have managed to get a six-syllable word into a hymn, but 'inextinguishable' will slow down any preacher, and 'can't be put out' is easier on the listeners.[32] Humpty Dumpty, in *Alice through the Looking Glass*, thought words could mean whatever he wanted them to, but (mercifully) he didn't write sermons, which are not the place to invent words or extend their meanings. Avoid repeating the same word too often unless it is essential; a thesaurus (start with the one on the computer) will suggest useful alternatives that add variety and depth. Use it, too, to replace weak words with stronger ones to add life. Keep sermons vibrant by preferring verbs to nouns (they are more active) and don't overload either with adverbs and adjectives, although they can aid visualization: Mark invites us to use our imaginations when he tells us that the grass at the feeding of the five thousand was green, and we can give similar sensory clues too, so instead of referring to someone picking a flower, why not describe it as a red rose? Instead of someone being angry, 'he slammed the door' is much more vivid. But beware of overloading with details: there can be so many adjectives that the noun is lost, so many adverbs that the verb is lost. Some words sound like the thing they want to convey, so let rain splosh rather than fall, the fighting be hostile or ferocious rather than heavy, the sound raucous or a cacophony rather than loud.

Another group of words that don't belong in sermons unless they can be justified are 'ought', 'should' 'need to' and 'must'. They smack of authoritarianism, and the congregation will feel browbeaten rather than exhorted and will miss the impact when we really do mean 'must'. Instead, invite people to imagine what happens if they do the thing we advocate. So, rather than say at the end of a sermon, 'We need to go into the world and preach the gospel', an imperative that is disempowering because it is so general, how much more vivid and inviting it is to say, 'Imagine what could happen if each one of us does one thing this week that shows God's love in action?' Apart from being more tantalizing to listen to, it is more enticing to action.

Over the last 40 years most people have caught on to inclusive language, but there are lingering traces of unnecessary masculine language. The Authorized Version uses 'man' and 'men' because when it was translated those words carried a wider sense of 'person', and changing the language when that translation is read violates the text. However, when preaching, we use contemporary language, and non-inclusive language will alienate most of the congregation, who take inclusive language for granted and for whom 'man' refers to the male of the species. This is in part due to the feminist influence, but also to the fact that people are losing the ability to think in metaphors, so hear as literal what was once metaphorical. As an example, after one sermon in which I referred to angels working overtime, an English lecturer thanked me for the poetic image while two other people told me they had discussed what I said and thought I was wrong to suggest angels exist in time. We need to be aware, too, of the damage that can be done if we use blindness as a metaphor for ignorance or blackness for sin.[33]

Now, check that we have written for speech rather than reading. I find that I slip naturally into 'oral speech mode' when writing a sermon and out of it again when I go back to writing for reading. How long and complex are sentences? Subordinate clauses do not belong in sermons, so make two sentences out of one and the congregation will thank us for it. At school I was taught never to begin a sentence with 'and' or 'but', but when speaking we have to give ourselves permission to break some of the rules of written English, so start sentences with 'and' or 'but' or any of the other words that make English teachers wince but are part of normal speech. Avoid 'however' and 'nevertheless' at the beginning of sentences because they belong in essays.

Avoid combinations of words that are hard to say one after another. For example, the sounds 'k', 'x', 'ct', 'st' take effort to articulate clearly when they are juxtaposed ('make clean', 'make straight', 'expects strong', 'first stage'), while 'verses four to six' is easier than 'fourth, fifth and sixth verses'. Be aware of words where it is tempting to slur or omit vowel sounds ('abs'lute' or 'conv'lute', 'pr'limin'ry', 'extr'ord'n'ry'). Sentences ending on unaccented syllables have diminished impact; it is better to say 'we greet him with joy' than 'we greet him joyfully'. The aim is for speech that is easy to say and pleasant to hear. If the sermon does not flow, check which words are causing the problem and replace them with alternatives. For that reason it is helpful to know something about the structure of poetry.[34]

Having done all of this, double-check the sermon for any hidden explosives: will something touch a raw nerve and so distract people that they cease listening or immediately bring their own interpretation and misunderstand you entirely? Problematic subjects already mentioned include abortion, suicide and sexuality issues, but there are more local ones, perhaps a divisive situation in the local area or an issue that is still raw and needs to be addressed directly and pastorally rather than as an illustration for something else.

Finally, lay the sermon out. The answer to dull reading of a full text is not to abandon a script but to lay it out so we can refer to it and maintain eye contact (preachers who are being filmed need to look at the camera not at the people). Underlining key words or phrases, bullet points, indented sub-sections of main points, or bold summary headings with the full text following each, can all help to make scripts hearer-friendly by giving us the confidence to look up at the congregation without getting lost when we glance at the script again to take in the next lines. Personally I have a full script in 12pt font, one and a half spacing, on A5 paper.

If someone wants to preach without a script, write out the opening and final sentences so that the sermon starts and finishes firmly. People who preach without notes usually have the headings and key moves mapped out and committed to memory beforehand, but even then a surprising number get the words in the wrong order when speaking. Memorizing the whole sermon is very time-consuming but for some people it can be a lifeline; I met one person who stammered when reading, but he learned his sermons and preached without any stammer at all.

Print out the script the day before preaching in case there is a power cut or the server goes down. Number the pages – one day we'll drop them. Read it aloud, even practise preaching it because even politicians can be caught out by phrases that they had not made their own, 'Sometimes (presidents making their inaugural speeches) appear baffled by the strange-tasting language they find in their own mouths . . . Lyndon Johnson haltingly read aloud [a] lyrical paean . . . his disbelief was audible.'[35] If possible when first beginning to preach, listen to the result on tape. Keep a record of sermons and index them by Scripture, date or theme. Include a note of where each sermon was preached. I do not advocate re-preaching sermons since, if our exegesis of the congregation is as faithful as our exegesis of the text, there is new work to be done on each new occasion. However, it can be helpful to refresh our memory of how we preached in the past and perhaps to borrow or adapt parts of the sermon for a new context.

Notes

1 Quoted in Charles Smyth, *The Art of Preaching: A Practical Survey of Preaching in the Church of England 747–1939*, SPCK, London, 1940, 1953, p. 176.

2 Phillips Brooks, *Lecture on Preaching (1877)*, H. R. Allenson, London, 1895, p. 172.

3 Durham Cathedral Sermons: 21 September 2008, 'Investment and Liberation', Canon Stephen Cherry.

4 Durham Cathedral Sermons: 27 July 2008, 'Angels in Confined Spaces', Canon Rosalind Brown.

5 Durham Cathedral Sermons: 8 June 2008, 'Suddenly', Canon Rosalind Brown.

6 Durham Cathedral Sermons: 13 April 2008, 'Unbinding Death', Canon David Kennedy.

7 Durham Cathedral Sermons: 29 March 2008, 'Thomas the Individual', Canon Stephen Cherry.

8 Durham Cathedral Sermons: 16 March 2008, 'The Humble Entry', Canon Stephen Cherry.

9 Durham Cathedral Sermons: 23 December 2007, 'Asked of the Lord', The Very Revd Michael Sadgrove.

10 Durham Cathedral Sermons: 11 March 2009, 'Farewell to Durham City Council', The Very Revd Michael Sadgrove.

11 Jonathan Rabin, 'The Golden Trumpet', in the *Guardian* Review Section, 24 January 2009, p. 2.

12 Durham Cathedral Sermons: 14 December 2008, 'Values for Advent – Joy', The Very Revd Michael Sadgrove.

13 Durham Cathedral Sermons: 2 November 2008, 'I Know that My Redeemer Liveth', Canon David Kennedy; 17 August 2008, 'Shouting at Jesus', Canon Stephen Cherry.

14 Durham Cathedral Sermons: 28 December 2008, 'Holy Innocents Day', Canon David Kennedy.

15 Durham Cathedral Sermons: 1 February 2009, 'Be Astounded! Be Very Astounded!', Canon Rosalind Brown.

16 Durham Cathedral Sermons: 24 August 2008, 'Following St Bartholomew's Example', Canon Rosalind Brown; 27 September 2008, 'A Welcome for Pilgrims', The Very Revd Michael Sadgrove.

17 Durham Cathedral Sermons: 19 May 2008, 'Trinity Sunday', Canon Rosalind Brown.

18 Durham Cathedral Sermons: 2 March 2008, 'Mustn't Grumble', Canon Stephen Cherry.

19 Lewis Carroll, *Alice's Adventures in Wonderland*, chapter 12.

20 William Sloane Coffin, quoted in John Killinger, *Fundamentals of Preaching*, SCM Press, London, 1985, pp. 92–3.

21 Durham Cathedral Sermons: 20 April 2008, 'Easter, Death and Life', Canon Rosalind Brown. The names have been changed.

22 Durham Cathedral Sermons: 23 March 2008, 'Out of Egypt', The Very Revd Michael Sadgrove.

23 Durham Cathedral Sermons: 16 March 2008, 'The Humble Entry', Canon Stephen Cherry.

24 Durham Cathedral Sermons: 23 December 2007, 'Asked of the Lord', The Very Revd Michael Sadgrove.

25 Durham Cathedral Sermons: 18 November 2007, 'Daniel and the Parable of the Sower', Canon Rosalind Brown.

26 Durham Cathedral Sermons: 1 March 2009, 'Stories About Being Human', Canon Rosalind Brown.

27 Durham Cathedral Sermons: 2 November 2005, 'Lacrimosa', The Very Revd Michael Sadgrove.

28 Remember that poetry and hymns are automatically in copyright until 70 years after the author's death and permission is always needed to quote even a few words in writing, whereas short extracts of prose can normally be quoted without specific permission so long as copyright is acknowledged. With the increased publication of sermons on the web, it is good practice to write to obtain permission before borrowing from them. Roman Catholic priests in Poland are, apparently, risking a fine or three-year prison sentence for copying sermons from the web without acknowledgement. See 'A tangled web in the pulpit', *Church Times*, 14 March 2008, p. 9.

29 Malcolm Gladwin, in his book *The Sticking Point*, quoted in William Leith's review of *Made to Stick: How Some Ideas Take Hold and Others Come Unstuck* by Chip and Dan Heath. The *Guardian* Review section, 24 February 2007.

30 William Shakespeare, *Hamlet*, Act 2, Scene 2, line 90. The following, less quoted line adds, 'and tediousness the limbs and outward flourishes'. Beware outward flourishes in sermons!

31 For further hints on editing the sermon for the ear, see G. Robert Jacks, *Just Say the Word: Writing for the Ear*, Eerdmans, Cambridge, 1996, and Richard G. Jones, *Groundwork of Worship and Preaching*, Epworth Press, London, 1980.

32 Research shows that the vocabulary of an average American 14-year-old has reduced from 24,000 words in 1950 to 10,000 by 2000. Quoted by Dr Tim Gorringe speaking in Salisbury, 13 October 2007.

33 See John Hull, 'Sight to the Inly Blind'? Attitude to Blindness in the Hymnbook', *Theology* 105, no. 827 (October 2002), pp. 333–41.

34 A good introduction can be found in Stephen Fry's enjoyable book, *The Ode Less Travelled*, Hutchinson, London, 2005.

35 Rabin, 'The Golden Trumpet', pp. 2–3. Presidents use speech writers, but we can easily be caught out by our own unfamiliar-sounding words.

10

PREACHING THE SERMON

Expressing our Wonder

It has been written of the actress who played the switchboard girl in Z *Cars* in the 1960s that her principal line, '"BD to Z Victor One" was memorably euphonious because she had worked hard to discover the poetry in the phrasing'.[1] All that work for one line! In contrast, John Newton's preaching was memorable for the wrong reasons:

> He admits that some were pleased, but many were disgusted by his efforts. He was thought 'too long, too loud, too much extempore.' He tried to redress this but preaching was never to be Newton's greatest strength. We are told that, though his personality and intense earnestness always commanded attention, the effect was spoilt by his poor delivery and awkward gestures.[2]

Delivery can make or break the impact of a sermon.

I was once at a dinner party sitting opposite a retired bishop who, when he discovered that I trained people for ordination, asked if we heard our students preach. I replied that we heard some but mostly had to rely on the local training ministers to do it. He was not impressed and then added in a loud voice, 'Do you know what the death of good preaching is? The invention of the shower!' That stopped the entire dinner party in its tracks and all eyes turned in our direction. He explained his theory that in the days before showers, clergy took a bath on Saturday night and declaimed their sermon to the bath taps, thereby honing their presentation and ensuring it was in their memory. With the invention of the shower, this was no longer possible and led to clergy mumbling away in the pulpit to no effect whatsoever.

Whatever the truth of his theory, it is true that even the best sermons lose their power by poor delivery. As a child I remember regularly counting the number of times the Vicar said 'Um' in a sermon; a habit I now know could be cured. Breath control is important, but when we are nervous that is one of the first things to go wrong, so a deep breath before speaking is needed and breathing exercises during the week will help. Many sermons are spoiled by weak technique, but help is available; the actor and preacher Geoffrey Stevenson has published very practical advice on the use and care of our voices,[3] and it may be worth seeking advice from an actor or someone used to public speaking, or getting a few elocution lessons. Failing all else, study the way people speak on the TV news. When I preach in other churches, I am shocked at the number of people who say, 'It was so refreshing to be able to hear what you said' as though that was a rare event. Volume can be checked before the service with someone else's help, but diction, pitch, inflection and speed need to be taken into account – the latter needs to be determined afresh for every building. If we mumble into a microphone all that will happen is that the congregation hears a louder mumbling. Buildings absorb sound differently, so check the acoustics, whether or not there is a sound system.

The relationship with this particular congregation on this particular day is vital, so establish eye contact with them from the start and begin with confidence so that they can respond with confidence in us. We have already been worshipping with the congregation and the sermon is a continuation of that worship, so we do not need to draw attention to ourselves when we enter the pulpit. We are there as the Church's preacher and not as an individual. However, if we are a visitor a brief opening comment might be appropriate, but this is not the time for an autobiography: the aim is to establish rapport with the congregation before leading them on the sermon's journey. Authority rather than authoritarianism is needed and our style should be appropriate to the occasion; the pulpit is not a place for delivery appropriate to a chat round the kitchen table and, even when standing among a small congregation we know, this is public worship and our choice of words and manner of delivery should be guided by that context, otherwise there is a lack of fit which jars. Similarly our manner of speaking should be natural, avoiding false religiosity, pomposity or affectation as well as declamation: they are all off-putting for the hearers, who will stop listening to the words. The great actress Dame Sybil Thorndike said, when referring to the effect of an audience on an actor, 'The quality of the audience makes all the difference in the world.'[4] Nurture that quality. To aid confidence, fledgling preachers can ask a friend to sit towards the back of the church and give feedback during the sermon in their body language. Then preach to that person, responding to their responses; this keeps our eyes up and on the congregation not our notes, and others in the congregation will pick up on our engagement with them. In particular, friends should smile at the preacher in order to encourage the preacher to smile back because that affects delivery and makes us more accessible to our hearers.

Posture affects delivery. If we look apologetic for being in the pulpit we will sound apologetic: we have been given authority to be there and our bearing should reflect that. Stand still without being rigid (wriggling and pacing to and fro are annoying to watch, but ramrod straightness is artificial) with feet about six to nine inches apart, shoulders back and down and head up. It sounds like drill but will become natural. Hands and arms should be ready for appropriate use, at our side or resting on (not grasping) the pulpit or lectern, never in pockets, folded or clasped behind our back. Gesture is important and should be natural and appropriate for us, for the space and for the expectations of the people; I find that automatically I gesture less when in the Cathedral pulpit, where large gestures are needed if they are to be seen, than in a smaller church, where my hands move more naturally with the rhythm of what I am saying. Every preacher should see themselves on video at least once, but it takes determination not over-react to the shock of seeing hitherto unknown mannerisms – they may not be inappropriate but, if they are, being conscious of them for ourselves is half the battle of dealing with them. Read a book on body language and seek the honest advice of a trusted friend, because body language, from wagging the finger to avoidance of eye contact, can send subtle and unintended messages, and if there is a lack of coherence between our words and our bodies, people will read our bodies.

It is important to respect the arrangement of space in the church, since it shapes worship and the congregation is familiar with it; if we disrupt it without consent we may lose the opportunity to challenge the congregation on other things. Most opposition to pulpits comes from preachers not congregations, and this fear of the pulpit by preachers is, I suspect, false humility about being six feet above contradiction and distanced from the congregation. Pulpits are there for practical reasons. They enable the congregation to hear and see the preacher and may have a microphone attached to a loop system. There is a strong functional argument for using them whether we like them or not, particularly if the congregation insists on sitting towards the back of the church, where their sight lines may be better than close to the pulpit. If we fear we are being distanced more than physically, that is a separate issue about our wider relationship with the congregation. With a small congregation sitting towards the front of the church, the chancel steps may be equally appropriate so long as we can still be seen and heard. Wandering up and down the aisle may boost a preacher's sense of contact with the congregation, but they may not share the feeling when they hear half the sermon from behind both their own and the preacher's backs. Apart from it being discourteous to talk to people with our backs to them, facial expressions and gestures can't be read from behind, and for people who lip-read this is a disaster.

Bad timing can ruin the effect: just as music has rests so speech needs rests, but it is very hard to have the confidence to keep silence in the pulpit. If necessary write a note to keep a rest. Pauses are needed when changing subjects or moods, to let something significant sink in, and to increase suspense – listen to storytellers and to the way comedians sometimes keep a long pause during which the audience gets the joke and starts laughing in anticipation of the punchline. In preaching, the art is to lead people to reach our conclusion for themselves.

Both rhetorical theory and experience tell us that the best sermon in the world cannot take wings if it has poor delivery; everything can be wasted if we fail to give attention to this aspect of preaching, which is often treated as a poor relation to the content of the sermon. Finally, ask people for honest feedback; it may be uncomfortable to hear but it is helpful. This can be done individually or in a group, perhaps over coffee after the service. The danger is that our friends will be over-eager to encourage us and miss out on constructive comments so it may be necessary to give them specific questions to talk to us about. Keep the emphasis on how this sermon can grow and develop, rather than whether it was 'good' or 'bad', which are very subjective responses. Examples of questions to ask hearers could include,

What was the sermon about? (its focus)
What did you take from the sermon? What effect will it have on you in the days to come? (its function)
How did it start? Did the preacher engage your attention?
Was it easy to follow? If so, why? If not, why not?
Did your attention wander? If so, when did this occur and do you know what might have caused it to happen?
What can you remember from the sermon?
Were you expecting it to end when it did? Do you know why this was?
Was the preacher easy to look at, or were there distracting mannerisms?
What do you want to say to encourage the preacher?

What constructive suggestions do you have for the preacher, or suggestions to try out in future?

To sum up, the keys to effective delivery of the sermon lie in being confident in what we have to say and in the way we will say it, being familiar with the text so that when preaching we are not caught out by something we had forgotten about, being visible and audible to the congregation and aware of how to use our voice in that particular space, and being ourselves open to the Holy Spirit. We preach because we love God and love people – that should come through in our tone of voice and our message. Theologically, it is about being prepared to preach as people called to proclaim the good news of God in a world that desperately needs to hear it, that wants to sing the Lord's song in whichever land they find themselves.

Timothy Radcliffe writes of the liturgical act of placing the gifts on the altar:

> In this moment of the liturgy we surrender ourselves to the gravitational pull of God's love, and swing around the apogee of our journey and are carried homewards ... We are like the three wise men who have given their gifts to Jesus. Because their hands are empty, they are free to accept whatever else God will give them, unlike Herod who sees the child as a threat to his possessions, his kingship and wealth. His hands are too full to receive the gift that he too is offered in Christ. We have placed everything on the altar in trust and hope, and so our hands are open to receive God's gifts, the body and blood of his Son.[5]

Preaching in the context of worship is a literal and metaphorical placing of our gifts on the altar which frees us, alongside those who hear us, to open our hands to receive from God. It is the fruit of our labour and our prayerful offering of ourselves and our version of the Lord's song as we stand, vulnerable, before the God who himself proclaimed that the kingdom of heaven is at hand.

Notes

1 Nigel Richardson, *Breakfast in Brighton*, Indigo Paperback, London, 1998, p. 11.

2 Sibyl Phillips, 'When Jesus Claims the Sinner's Heart, John Newton (1725–1807): From Infidel to Olney Hymn Writer. Part 2', *Bulletin of the Hymn Society of Great Britain and Ireland* 18.9 (January 2008), p. 300.

3 Geoffrey Stevenson and Stephen Wright, *Preaching with Humanity: A Practical Guide for Today's Church*, Church House Publishing, London, 2008, pp. 82ff. See also Richard G. Jones, *Groundwork of Worship and Preaching*, Epworth Press, London, 1980, pp. 214ff.

4 Donald Coggan, *Stewards of Grace*, Hodder & Stoughton, London, 1958, p. 87.

5 Timothy Radcliffe, *Why go to Church?* Continuum, London, 2008, p. 106.

II

HOW CAN WE SING
THE LORD'S SONG IN
A FOREIGN LAND?

*A sermon preached at a vocation and ministry training
weekend for recently ordained clergy in the Dioceses of
Blackburn and Carlisle. 15 March 2009*

Psalm 137; John 2.13–22

How could we sing the LORD's song in a foreign land?

Come with me to meet the psalmists. They are in exile in
Babylon and many of their friends have abandoned the faith
that defined them as a people; perhaps overawed by the sheer
magnificence of Babylon, which made Jerusalem as they remembered it seem puny in comparison, they had concluded that the
gods of Babylon were better than the God of Israel at looking
after their followers. It is very easy to slip into doubting God
when life turns sour on us. But others have remained faithful
to their God and we find some of them sitting and weeping
on the riverbanks, reminded all too harshly that this is alien
territory – they were used to the rugged hills of Judaea and
here all is sandy and flat, horribly flat, with vistas reaching into
the distance instead of the enclosure of their beloved mountains. Their physical surroundings, their emotional distress, the
pagan culture around them: all shriek 'exile'.

Worse, this exile has eaten into their souls. These singers, who might have been the musicians from the temple in Jerusalem and have carried their harps into exile hoping to continue to lead the people in worship, have concluded there is no hope and have hung up their harps. Their captors are insisting they sing their sacred songs as entertainment: this is more than playing Strauss waltzes at the entrance to Auschwitz, it is turning their Hallelujah Chorus into a comedy act at the enemy's Royal Variety Performance. Rather than prostitute themselves in this way they have simply given up the unequal task of keeping the nation's faith alive through song. And now, gathered by the river whose waters do not restore their souls, these distressed singers face their failure head-on. All their ambitions have come to nothing, life is against them; unthinkably, perhaps even God is against them. Why not just give up on God as their compatriots have done?

Instead they ask a question: 'How can we sing the Lord's song in a foreign land?' On the face of it, it is an admission of abject failure. How can we sing? The straightforward answer is, 'We can't.' But then they go on: 'If I forget you, O Jerusalem, let my right hand – the hand I use to play my harp – wither! Let my tongue cling to the roof of my mouth – let me be dumb – if I do not remember you, if I do not set Jerusalem above my highest joy.' They are determined not to forget. So perhaps the question is not so much a rhetorical question as a genuine probing search: it is not 'Can we or can't we sing the Lord's song in a foreign land' but 'In what way can we sing it?'

That is a much more demanding question, but they are determined to pursue it. Amnesia is not an option for these exiles, their very identity is tied up in their remembering who they are and where they have come from. To know who they are as God's people they have to do the hard work of forging a new song out of devastation, out of exile, their memories of Jerusalem in ruins, the mocking of their conquerors, the infidelity of their fellow-countrymen, the fidelity of God.

And their first attempt at singing is one that is so uncomfortable to us that the lectionary brackets these verses, enabling us to omit them from our worship. This new song from exile is one that dredges up injustices done to them in the past. The Edomites, descended from Esau, Jacob's brother, had been their allies but then betrayed Judah to the Babylonians; the Babylonians had razed Jerusalem to the ground, burned it and left its streets running with blood before forcing the people taken into exile to carry its treasures on their backs for hundreds of miles, only to see their sacred objects put to pagan use. And now their pent-up anger is unleashed, 'O daughter Babylon, you devastator, happy shall they be who pay you back what you have done to us! Happy shall they be who take your little ones and dash them against the rock!' These are not noble sentiments, but perhaps we have to be sitting in the rubble (of Gaza?) to understand.

We have to put ourselves in their religious shoes as well. The previous psalm (136.10) cites the killing of the firstborn in Egypt as a sign of God's steadfast love, and it was not uncommon for victorious armies to kill children, especially boys, and with babies and young children they did this by dashing them on rocks. There are at least three references in the Bible to this happening, and there are parallel petitions in other psalms that call down equal horrors on their enemies. Without trying to justify the actions, we have to acknowledge that, within the conduct of war at the time, all the exiles are dreaming of is that the *lex talionis*, 'an eye for an eye', should operate. They are yearning for no more than that their enemies are paid back in equal measure. And they do not ask to do this themselves, they entrust their passion for vengeance to God in the only prayer in this psalm, 'Remember, O Lord, against the Edomites, the day of Jerusalem's fall.'

And it is in the midst of these terrible words at the end of the psalm that they begin to forge their own answer to their question. 'How can we sing the Lord's song in a foreign land?' How? By refusing to forget their past – their beloved city lying in ruins, their fellow countrymen killed in its streets – and turning to God again, learning that God is not a territorial god, as most nations thought their gods to be, but that God is with them in exile and can be entrusted with their passions; by doing the hard work of facing the horror and refusing the much simpler option of blaming God for abandoning them. No, the song they are to sing in this foreign land is still the Lord's song, and therefore it has to express their past and their present. They have to find a way to say, 'This is how we sing the Lord's song in the new circumstances in which we find ourselves.'

And, I suggest to you: that is at the heart of all ministry.

When we preach or offer pastoral care, when we teach or preside at the Eucharist, we are helping people to sing the Lord's song in a foreign land. That is obvious at funerals – people have been thrust into the uncharted territory of this particular bereavement and faith may be wavering – but it should be clear to us, if not to the congregation, whenever we preach and bring the world of the Bible into dialogue with the world of the twenty-first century. Our world today is a foreign land to the psalmists, but their song needs to ring out in contemporary language and contemporary society because, whatever else has changed, human nature and human experience have not. We have only to look at the TV to know that people are still forced into exile, homes are destroyed and children murdered by armies, that jobs and livelihoods are lost at a stroke by the actions of other people. If we look at our congregations, each week there are people – often looking fine on the outside – who face unemployment, the loss of life savings, divorce, drug addiction in their families, domestic violence from someone they trusted, failed exams. These are all foreign countries into which they are exiled, and their presence in church is a tacit plea that we help them to sing the Lord's song in this particular unknown territory.

Our task is to help them find the first note, to catch the melody, to remember the words. We cannot sing their song for them but we can hum enough for them to join in and then to create their own melodies, harmonies and descants; to sing the Lord's song in a strange land.

However, we must beware of being lulled into a false sense of security about the song of our faith: what was vibrant once can become sentimental crooning. There are always new songs to be learned, and in the Gospel reading Jesus turns things upside-down in the rebuilt temple. He is foreshadowing another exile from old religious securities by pointing, in an allusion that was not understood at the time, to his death and resurrection. Sometimes we will find ourselves speaking words that are not welcome, the prophetic words that challenge comfortable security, that invite people to leave the past behind and come with us on a journey that requires us to sing a new song in a foreign land. That, too, is part of the ministry with which we have been entrusted.

The foreign land may be thrust upon us unwillingly or may be the unexpected destination on a journey of discovery freely chosen. The psalmists by the rivers of Babylon remind us of the hard work of faith but assure us that there is indeed a new song to sing in a foreign land, and there is a first note to be found – indeed the Holy Spirit is always humming it to us if we will but listen.

'How can we sing the Lord's song in a foreign land?' What songs have you sung in a foreign land? Help your people to learn and to sing wonderful new harmonies and descants to the melody of God's faithful love. That is the challenge and the joy of ministry.

12

CAN WORDS EXPRESS OUR WONDER?

Why do we preach? Simply because we are called to care for the people of God.

What do we preach? We proclaim that the kingdom of heaven is at hand – all else flows from that.

Where do we preach? In worship, because there we stand with our hearers before God, open to the Holy Spirit's vivifying presence among us.

How do we preach? With wonder, with the very best we can offer from our life with God: we are first of all lovers of God and hearers of God's word.

> Your voice, O God, outsings the stars of morning,
> your art in sky and season is displayed,
> your complex ways we trace in awe and wonder,
> marvel that in your image we are made.
>
> What can we say? Can words express our wonder?
> How shall we live? Can we reflect your grace?
> Come Spirit, come, disturb our cautious living,
> be known in us, your human dwelling place.
>
> You call your church from every land and nation,
> you reconcile, for we in Christ are one.
> We yearn to see creation's full redemption
> all things restored in Christ the risen Son.

O holy God, we worship and adore you,
your Word made flesh shared human joy and strife,
in him you draw us in love's dance of freedom:
your church, your people, in your common life.[1]

Note

1 Copyright © 2003 Rosalind Brown. Tune: Highwood.